A

Nature Lover's

BOOK OF

Quotations

☾

A

Nature Lover's

BOOK OF

Quotations

COMPILED AND EDITED BY

TOM CRIDER

WOOD ENGRAVINGS BY

THOMAS W. NASON

BIRCH TREE PUBLISHING
SOUTHBURY, CT

First edition, 2000

Printed in Canada on recycled acid-free paper

BOOK DESIGN AND COMPOSITION BY BARBARA MARKS

Library of Congress Card Number: 00-190353

ISBN: 0-9679430-0-0

☾ contents

❡ introduction

It is in man's heart that the life
of nature's spectacle exists; to see it, one
must feel it.

—JEAN-JACQUES ROUSSEAU

This collection of quotations was
assembled by one nature lover for another—
you, dear reader. You will truly appreciate this
book if you are someone who feels, as Rousseau
says, the *life* of nature's spectacle; if you are
one to whom the birds, frogs, and trees are
more like kin than objects designed for your
entertainment or profit; and if you reject as
preposterous the notion that human beings are
separate from and superior to the natural world.
It's not easy being a nature lover these days.
Most of us spend too much time indoors, our
energies drained by duties considered more
urgent than hiking in the hills. Wordsworth

said it well: " . . . getting and spending we lay
waste our powers / Little we see in nature that is
ours." Keep this book handy. It will help keep
your feeling for nature alive.

What a pleasure it is to have something
you believe in expressed more eloquently
than you could say it yourself: "Destroying a
rainforest for economic gain is like burning a
Renaissance painting to cook a meal." (Edward
O. Wilson) Many quotations in this collection
do that. You'll also find some that distill an
idea with startling clarity, as John Muir's does:
"When we try to pick out anything by itself,
we find that it is hitched to everything else in
the universe." That's the essence of ecology,
isn't it?

For the most part, the quotations in this
book celebrate nature: "There is a pleasure in
the pathless woods / There is a rapture on the
lonely shore . . . " (Lord Byron) But if we over-
idealize nature, we distance ourselves from her.
In order to keep from becoming too starry-eyed,

we need, now and then, to be brought down to earth: "Nature is not a pretty, manicured place maintained for human beings. It is a dynamic continuum, often a violent one." (Dave Foreman) In these pages, you will even find, here and there, statements that reflect sharply opposing perspectives. I have included these because dissenting views can force a clearer focus. Of course, nature lovers themselves are not of one mind. You'll come across some, like Gerard Manley Hopkins, who see nature as "charged with the grandeur of God," while others, like Stephen Jay Gould, are more cerebral: "Nature is what she is—amoral and persistent." Scientists, poets, novelists, saints, philosophers, humorists, naturalists, and even astronauts, all with something of their own to say, are here to edify, delight, and sustain you.

This collection is fairly comprehensive, but is not meant to be a reference work. It's one person's carefully selected handful of stones, not all the stones on the beach. As for the way it's organized, I've assembled the quotations in categories that make sense to me, and I hope to you as well. Some, such as "Affinity" and "Kinship," are similar, so I suggest you return to the list in the front of the book after reading through one category if you yearn for more along the same line. The categories are arranged alphabetically, which gives the collection an arbitrary sort of order, but, rather than seeing this as a fault, I think it invites you to wander through the pages as you might walk through a forest, bending here and there to look closely at what catches your eye.

Within the categories you'll find various things happening. Some quotations are arranged chronologically, but more often they build upon one another or approach the subject from a slightly different angle. Still others disagree with each other, as when Einstein says, "God does not play dice with the universe," and Stephen Hawking retorts, "God not only plays dice, he throws the dice

where they cannot be seen." The Pilgrim leader
William Bradford speaks of the "hideous and
desolate wilderness, full of wild beasts and wild
men," and Chief Luther Standing Bear says,
"to us it was tame."

Because nature lovers can't help but be
disturbed and saddened by the abuse of nature
taking place all around us, I've included
quotations dealing with "Loss" and "Ruination,"
and put others under "Conservation" and
"Stewardship," which point to ways in which
nature can be treated with greater understanding
and respect. It would have been easy to overfill
these categories with hand-wringing, finger-
pointing, and preaching. However, although
there is ample justification for whole volumes
devoted to this sort of thing, I have tried to
provide just enough to offer a counterpoint to
the predominantly rhapsodic tone of the other
categories. It's not enough for us to celebrate
nature; as Plato says, we have to "take care of her
more carefully than children do their mother."

Winston Churchill said, "Quotations when engraved upon the memory give you good thoughts." You're sure to find many in these pages worth remembering, and I trust they will indeed give you good thoughts. Churchill also said that quotations make you want to read more of what the author wrote. This is sure to happen as well. The authors quoted here have written some wonderful books that will renew your enthusiasm and deepen your understanding. I urge you to consult the index for suggestions for further reading.

But, having said this, allow me to point out that, as Robert Louis Stevenson observed, "Books are good enough in their own way, but they are a mighty bloodless substitute for life." Or nature. There's no substitute for getting out there. May this book inspire you to open the door and walk out under that "vaulted sky" (John Clare) as often as you can.

—TOM CRIDER

A

Nature Lover's

BOOK OF

Quotations

☾

❪ affinity

There is a pleasure in the pathless woods,
There is a rapture on the lonely shore
There is society, where none intrudes,
By the deep Sea, and Music in its roar;
I love not Man the less, but Nature more.

—LORD BYRON

I am in love with this world. I have nestled lovingly in it. I have climbed its mountains, roamed its forests, sailed its waters, crossed its deserts, felt the sting of its frosts, the oppression of its heats, the drench of its rains, the fury of its winds, and always have beauty and joy waited upon my goings and comings.

—JOHN BURROUGHS

. . . Nature never did betray
The heart that loved her.

— WILLIAM WORDSWORTH

I long for scenes, where man hath never trod,
A place where woman never smiled or
wept—
There to abide with my Creator, God,
And Sleep as I in childhood sweetly slept,
Untroubling, and untroubled where I lie,
The grass below—above the vaulted sky.

— JOHN CLARE

Hold your hands out over the earth as over a flame. To all who love her, who open to her the doors of their veins, she gives of her strength, sustaining them.

— HENRY BESTON

The sounding cataract
Haunted me like a passion; the tall rock,
The mountain, and the deep and gloomy
    wood,
Their colours and their forms, were then
    to me
An appetite; a feeling and a love,
That had no need of a remoter charm,
By thought supplied, nor any interest
Unborrowed from the eye.

—WILLIAM WORDSWORTH

As long as I retain my feeling and my passion for Nature, I can partly soften or subdue my other passions and resist or endure those of others.

—LORD BYRON

There is delight in the hardy life of the open. There are no words that can tell the hidden spirit of the wilderness, that can reveal its mystery, its melancholy, and its charm.

—THEODORE ROOSEVELT

The old Lakota was wise. He knew that man's heart away from nature becomes hard; he knew that lack of respect for growing, living things soon led to lack of respect for humans too. So he kept his youth close to its softening influence.

—CHIEF LUTHER STANDING BEAR

Let children walk with Nature, let them see the beautiful blendings and communions of death and life, their joyous inseparable unity . . .

—JOHN MUIR

We can never get enough of nature. We must be refreshed by the sight of inexhaustible vigor, vast and titanic features, the sea-coast with its wrecks, the wilderness with its living and its decaying trees, the thundercloud, and the rain which lasts three weeks and produces freshets. We need to witness our own limits transgressed, and some life pasturing freely where we never wander.

— HENRY DAVID THOREAU

After you have exhausted what there is in business, politics, conviviality, and so on— have found that none of these finally satisfy, or permanently wear—what remains? Nature remains.

— WALT WHITMAN

« beauty

To the dull mind nature is leaden. To the illumined mind the whole world burns and sparkles with light.

— RALPH WALDO EMERSON

The hours when the mind is absorbed in beauty are the only hours when we truly live.

— RICHARD JEFFERIES

The greatest beauty is organic wholeness, the wholeness of life and things, the divine beauty of the universe. Love that, not man apart from that.

— ROBINSON JEFFERS

No synonym for God is so perfect as Beauty. Whether as seen carving the lines of the mountains with glaciers, or gathering matter into stars, or planning the movements of water, or gardening—still all is Beauty!

—JOHN MUIR

We may regard it as a favour that nature has extended to us, that besides giving us what is useful it has dispensed beauty and charms in such abundance, and for this we may love it, just as we view it with respect because of its immensity, and feel ourselves ennobled by such contemplation—just as if nature had erected and decorated its splendid stage with this precise purpose in its mind.

—IMMANUEL KANT

There is material enough in a single flower for the ornament of a score of cathedrals.

—JOHN RUSKIN

Our ability to perceive quality in nature begins, as in art, with the pretty. It expands through successive stages of the beautiful to values as yet uncaptured by language. The quality of cranes lies, I think, in this higher gamut, as yet beyond the reach of words.

—ALDO LEOPOLD

❦ being there

The naturalist must allow himself to be engulfed to his very ears in the odors and textures of sensible reality. He must become, like the muskrat, a limpid eyeball peering out of the sedges of a flooded meadow. By being fully immersed in his fluid environment as this sleek brown rodent, the naturalist could see his world with all his senses cleansed and alert.

—HENRY DAVID THOREAU

The man who has seen the rising moon break out of the clouds at midnight has been present like an archangel at the creation of light and of the world.

—RALPH WALDO EMERSON

I have often remarked that it is wise for a naturalist on the prowl to sit down on some mossy bank or other inviting ground for an hour or so. . . . Use your eyes as much as you can; open your ears to every sound, but make no movement and no noise. I was once sitting quietly on a hedge-bank, seeing many things to interest me, when a Hare came leisurely along a track, and actually jumped over my outstretched legs. I had never had so good a look at a Hare in a state of nature before. . . . I have even had butterflies settle on my coat and sun themselves there. Study to be quiet.

—CHARLES A. HALL

To those who have not yet learned the secret of true happiness, begin now to study the little things in your own dooryard.

—GEORGE WASHINGTON CARVER

To rest under a willow tree, bathed in the cool evening breeze, and watch the moon rising above the trees, is sufficient to drive away selfish desires, and uplift every thought.

— KAIBARA EKKEN

Night is a dead monotonous period under a roof; but in the open world it passes lightly, with its stars and dews and perfumes, and the hours are marked by changes in the face of Nature. What seems a kind of temporal death to people choked between walls and curtains is only a light and living slumber to the man who sleeps afield.

— ROBERT LOUIS STEVENSON

Most people are *on* the world, not in it—have no conscious sympathy or relationship to anything about them—undiffused, separate, and rigidly alone like marbles of polished stone, touching but separate.

—JOHN MUIR

. . . Unless the soul goes out to meet what we see we do not see it; nothing do we see, not a beetle, not a blade of grass.

—WILLIAM HENRY HUDSON

The book of nature is like a page written over or printed upon with different-sized characters and in many different languages . . . and with a great variety of references . . . It is a book which he reads best who goes most slowly or even tarries long by the way.

—JOHN BURROUGHS

And leaning on my elbow and my side,
The long day I shope me for to abyde,
For nothing els, and I shal not lie
But for to look upon the daisie,
That well by reason men it calle may
The daisie, or els the eye of the day,
The Emprisse and floure of floures all.

—GEOFFREY CHAUCER

The marsh, to him who enters it in a receptive mood, holds, besides mosquitoes and stagnation, melody, the mystery of unknown waters, and the sweetness of Nature undisturbed by man.

—CHARLES WILLIAM BEEBE

Never have my thoughts been more devoutly raised to Heaven, than in some of our rambles through these magnificent forests; especially of an evening, when we have prepared our bed of dried leaves, under the canopy of a branching oak, or a lofty pine; the moon's silver rays casting a modest light through the trees, and the whip-poor-will lulling us with his melancholy note to sleep . . .

—PRISCILLA WAKEFIELD

Travel by canoe is not a necessity, and will nevermore be the most efficient way to get from one region to another, or even from one lake to another—anywhere. A canoe trip has become simply a rite of oneness with certain terrain, a diversion off the field, an art performed not because it is a necessity but because there is value in the art itself.

—JOHN MCPHEE

When I dance, I dance; when I sleep, I sleep; yes, and when I walk alone in a beautiful orchard, if my thoughts drift to far-off matters for some part of the time, for some other part I lead them back again to the walk, the orchard, to the sweetness of this solitude, to myself.

—MICHEL DE MONTAIGNE

It is a remarkably pleasant occupation, to lie on one's back in a forest and look upwards! It seems that you are looking into a bottomless sea, that it is stretching out far and wide *below* you, that the trees are not rising from the earth but, as if they were the roots of enormous plants, are descending or falling steeply into those lucid, glassy waves.

— IVAN TURGENEV

It seems to me that we all look at Nature too much, and live with her too little.

— OSCAR WILDE

You are sitting on the earth and you realize that this earth deserves you and you deserve this earth. You are there—fully, personally, genuinely.

— CHOGYAM TRUNGPA

I sat there listening with my
whole being, and with my whole strength
contemplating that mountain that I so dearly
love. . . . Was there anyone in the world, at
that moment, as happy as I?

— COLETTE RICHARD

If the doors of perception were cleansed
every thing would appear to man as it is—
infinite.

— WILLIAM BLAKE

How describe the delicate thing that
happens when a brilliant insect alights on a
flower? Words, with their weight, fall upon the
picture like birds of prey.

— JULES RENARD

There came a sudden avalanche
of tropical rain, crashing to earth, and
immediately, in a small stream, small fish like
sunfish leaped and whirled. A water snake,
emerald-speckled on a throat distended by
what must have been a still-live frog, swam
clumsily away, disappearing into a black tunnel
where the stream slipped into the jungle wall;
at this moment, for the first time, the jungle
came into focus for me. I could feel it, hear
it, smell it all at once, could believe I was
almost there.

—PETER MATTHIESSEN

We must go out and re-ally ourselves to
Nature every day. We must take root, send out
some little fibre at least, even every winter day.

—HENRY DAVID THOREAU

By such a river it is impossible to believe that one will ever be tired or old. Every sense applauds it. Taste it, feel its chill on the teeth: it is purity absolute.

— WALLACE STEGNER

The quieter you become the more you can hear.

— RAM DASS

... We regard all created beings as sacred and important, for everything has a *wochangi*, or influence, which can be given to us, through which we may gain a little more understanding, if we are attentive.

—BLACK ELK

To really experience the desert you have to march right into its white bowl of sky and shape-contorting heat with your mind on your canteen as if it were your last gallon of gas and you were being chased by a carload of escaped murderers. You have to imagine what it would be like to drink blood from a lizard or, in the grip of dementia, claw bare-handed through sand and rock for the vestigial moisture beneath a dry wash.

—MARC REISNER

What I aim to do is not so much learn the names of the shreds of creation that flourish in this valley, but to . . . keep myself open to their meanings, which is to try to impress myself at all times with the fullest possible force of their very reality. I want to have things as multiply and intricately as possible present and visible in my mind. Then I might be able to sit on the hill by the burnt books where the starlings fly over, and see not only the starlings, the grass field, the quarried rock, the viney woods, Hollins Pond, and the mountains beyond, but also, and simultaneously, feathers' barbs, springtails in the soil, crystal in rock, chloroplasts streaming, rotifers pulsing, and the shape of the air in the pines.

—ANNIE DILLARD

❨ connections

When we try to pick out anything by itself, we find that it is hitched to everything else in the universe.

—JOHN MUIR

Nature is the nature of all things that are; things that are have a union with all things from the beginning.

—MARCUS AURELIUS

No man is an island, entire of itself; every man is a piece of the continent, a part of the whole.

—JOHN DONNE

Nature is one connected whole. At any given moment every part must be precisely what it is, because all other parts are what they are, and not a grain of sand could be moved from its place without changing something throughout all parts of the immeasurable whole.

—JOHANN GOTTLIEB FICHTE

To see a world in a grain of sand
And a heaven in a wild flower,
Hold infinity in the palm of your hand
And eternity in an hour.

—WILLIAM BLAKE

This earth which is spread out like a map around me is but the lining of my inmost soul exposed.

—HENRY DAVID THOREAU

Let a man once begin to think about the mystery of his life and the links which connect him with the life that fills the world, and he cannot but bring to bear upon his own life and all other life that comes within his reach the principle of reverence for life . . .

—ALBERT SCHWEITZER

Each portion of matter may be conceived of as a garden full of plants, and as a pond full of fishes. But each branch of the plant, each member of the animal, each drop of its humors, is also such a garden or such a pond.

—GOTTFRIED WILHELM VON LEIBNIZ

The first law of ecology is that everything is related to everything else.

—BARRY COMMONER

Quantum theory thus reveals a basic oneness of the universe. . . . As we penetrate into matter, nature does not show us any isolated "basic building blocks," but rather appears as a complicated web of relations between the various parts of the whole.

— FRITJOF CAPRA

With all beings and all things we shall be as relatives.

— BLACK ELK

The whole universe is endowed with the same breath, rocks, trees, grass, earth, all animals and men.

— HOPI SAYING

The lakes and rivers sustain us; they flow through the veins of the earth and into our own.

—ALBERT GORE

Flower in the crannied wall,
I pluck you out of the crannies,
I hold you here, root and all, in my hand,
Little flower—but if I could understand
What you are, root and all, and all in all,
I should know what God and man is.

—ALFRED, LORD TENNYSON

In the skin of our fingers we can see the trail of the wind; it shows us where the wind blew when our ancestors were created.

—NAVAJO LEGEND

Whatever befalls the earth befalls the sons of the earth. Man did not weave the web of life; he is merely a strand in it. Whatever he does to the web, he does to himself.

—CHIEF SEATTLE

The universe is bound together in communion, each thing with all the rest. The gravitational bond unites all the galaxies; the electromagnetic interaction binds all the molecules; the genetic information connects all the generations of the ancestral tree of life. We live in interwoven layers of bondedness.

—BRIAN SWIMME

Thou canst not stir a flower
Without troubling of a star.

—FRANCIS THOMPSON

Every individual is an expression of the whole realm of nature, a unique action of the total universe.

—ALAN WATTS

I believe a leaf of grass is no less than the journeywork of the stars.

—WALT WHITMAN

In our infancy as a species, we felt no separation from the natural world around us. Trees, rocks, and plants surrounded us with a living presence as intimate and pulsing as our own bodies. . . . Now . . . having gained distance and sophistication of perception, we can turn and recognize who we have been all along . . . we are our world knowing itself.

—JOANNA MACY

The deep ecology sense of self-realization goes beyond the modern Western sense of "self" as an isolated ego striving for hedonistic gratification. . . . Self, in this sense, is experienced as integrated with the whole of nature.

—BILL DEVALL AND GEORGE SESSIONS

All ethics so far evolved rest upon a single premise: that the individual is a member of a community of interdependent parts. His instincts prompt him to compete for his place in the community, but his ethics prompt him also to co-operate (perhaps in order that there may be a place to compete for).

The land ethic simply enlarges the boundaries of the community to include soils, waters, plants, and animals, or collectively: the land.

—ALDO LEOPOLD

☾ conservation

Since the land is the parent, let the citizens take care of her more carefully than children do their mother.

—PLATO

That which is not good for the beehive cannot be good for the bees.

—MARCUS AURELIUS

As for those who would take the world
To alter it as they see fit,
I observe that they never succeed:
For the world is a sacred vessel
Not made to be altered by man.
The tinkerer will spoil it;
Usurpers will lose it.

—LAO TSU

Earth gives life and seeks the man who walks gently upon it.

—HOPI SAYING

The earth is not ours, it is a treasure we hold in trust for future generations.

—AFRICAN PROVERB

Nothing was made by God for man to spoil or destroy.

—JOHN LOCKE

Conservation is a state of harmony between men and land.

—ALDO LEOPOLD

A grove of giant redwoods or sequoias should be kept just as we keep a great or beautiful cathedral.

— THEODORE ROOSEVELT

Let us give Nature a chance; she understands her business better than we do.

— MICHEL DE MONTAIGNE

In one respect every natural area has a common uniqueness—it takes everyone forever to preserve it, but one person and one time to destroy it.

— E. J. KOESTNER

Let me ask you this—why are there only eight inches of topsoil left in America, when there were some 18 inches at the time of the Declaration of Independence in 1776? Where goes our sacred earth?

—HOBART KEITH

The frog does not drink up the pond in which he lives.

—AMERICAN INDIAN PROVERB

Conservation is sometimes perceived as stopping everything cold, as holding whooping cranes in higher esteem than people. It is up to science to spread the understanding that the choice is not between wild places or people, it is between a rich or an impoverished existence for Man.

—THOMAS LOVEJOY

The long fight to save wild beauty represents democracy at its best. It requires citizens to practice the hardest of virtues—self- restraint.

—EDWIN WAY TEALE

On Spaceship Earth there are no passengers; everybody is a member of the crew. We have moved into an age in which everybody's activities affect everybody else.

—MARSHALL MCLUHAN

Something will have gone out of us as a people if we ever let the remaining wilderness be destroyed; if we permit the last virgin forests to be turned into comic books and plastic cigarette cases; if we drive the few remaining members of the wild species into zoos or to extinction; if we pollute the last clear air and dirty the last clean streams and push our paved roads through the last of the silence, so that never again will Americans be free in their own country from the noise, the exhausts, the stinks of human and automotive waste. And so that never again can we have the chance to see ourselves single, separate, vertical and individual in the world, part of the environment of trees and rocks and soil, brother to the other animals, part of the natural world and competent to belong in it.

—WALLACE STEGNER

Man has sufficient objective reasons to cling to the safe-keeping of the wild world. But nature will only be saved after all by our hearts.

—JEAN DORST

Environmentalists make terrible neighbors but great ancestors.

—DAVID R. BROWER

Conservation is humanity caring for the future.

—NANCY NEWHALL

We have lived by the assumption that what was good for us would be good for the world. We have been wrong. We must change our lives, so that it will be possible to live by the contrary assumption that what is good for the world will be good for us. And that requires that we make the effort to know the world and to learn what is good for it. We must learn to cooperate in its processes, and to yield to its limits. But even more important, we must learn to acknowledge that the creation is full of mystery; we will never clearly understand it. We must abandon arrogance and stand in awe. We must recover the sense of the majesty of the creation, and the ability to be worshipful in its presence. For it is only on the condition of humility and reverence before the world that our species will be able to remain in it.

—WENDELL BERRY

☾ creatures

If indeed thy heart were right, then would every creature be to thee a mirror of life, and a book of holy doctrine.

—THOMAS À KEMPIS

Tiger! Tiger! burning bright
In the forests of the night,
What immortal hand or eye
Could frame thy fearful symmetry?

—WILLIAM BLAKE

Nature is to be found in her entirety nowhere more than in her smallest creatures.

—PLINY THE ELDER

For that which befalleth the sons of men befalleth beasts; even one thing befalleth them: as the one dieth, so dieth the other; yea, they have all one breath; so that a man hath no preeminence above a beast. . . . All go unto one place; all are of the dust, and all turn to dust again. Who knoweth the spirit of man that goeth upward, and the spirit of the beast that goeth downward to the earth?

—BIBLE, *ECCLESIASTES* 3:19–21

It is not with respect to our convenience or discomfort, but with respect to their own nature, that the creatures are glorifying to their Maker.

—SAINT AUGUSTINE OF HIPPO

Indeed what reason may not goe to Schoole to the wisedome of Bees, Ants, and Spiders? what wise hand teacheth them to doe what reason cannot teach us?

— THOMAS BROWNE

Love animals, God has given them the rudiments of thought and joy untroubled. Do not trouble their joy, don't harass them; don't deprive them of their happiness.

— FYODOR DOSTOEVSKY

If there is a just God, how humanity would writhe in its attempt to justify its treatment of animals.

— ISAAC ASIMOV

God loved the birds and invented trees.
Man loved the birds and invented cages.

—JACQUES DEVAL

Learn from the birds what food the thickets
*   yield;*
Learn from the beasts the physic of the field;
The arts of building from the bee receive;
Learn of the mole to plow, the worm to
*   weave.*

—ALEXANDER POPE

In a dogwood's petaled salon, bees leave
their pollen footprints as calling cards.

—DIANE ACKERMAN

And that was another gap between us. Between all men and all insects. We humans, saddled for a lifetime with virtually the same body, naturally find it difficult to imagine a life in which you can, at a single stroke, outside a fairy tale, just by splitting your skin and stepping out, change into something utterly different.

—COLIN FLETCHER

The butterfly counts not months but
moments,
And has time enough.

—RABINDRANATH TAGORE

I go about looking at horses and cattle. They eat grass, make love, work when they have to, bear their young. I am sick with envy of them.

—SHERWOOD ANDERSON

We patronize them for their incompleteness, for their tragic fate of having taken form so far below ourselves. And therein we err, and greatly err. For the animal shall not be measured by man. In a world older and more complete than ours they move finished and complete, gifted with extensions of the senses we have lost or never attained, living by voices we shall never hear. They are not brethren, they are not underlings; they are other nations, caught with ourselves in the net of life and time, fellow prisoners of the splendor and travail of the earth.

— HENRY BESTON

We have enslaved the rest of the animal creation, and have treated our distant cousins in fur and feathers so badly that beyond doubt, if they were able to formulate a religion, they would depict the Devil in human form.

— WILLIAM RALPH INGE

The greatness of a nation and its moral progress can be judged by the way its animals are treated.

—MOHANDAS GANDHI

Lady butterfly
Perfumes her wings by floating
Over the orchid.

—BASHŌ

We others. . . have only the word "smell". . . to include the whole range of delicate thrills which murmur in the nose of the animal night and day, summoning, warning, inciting, repelling.

—KENNETH GRAHAME

Deer, otter, foxes are messengers from another condition of life, another mentality, and bring us tidings of places where we don't go.

—EDWARD HOAGLAND

An animal, whether real or imaginary, has a place of honor in the sphere of the imagination. As soon as it is named it takes on a dreamlike power, becoming an allegory, a symbol, an emblem.

—ITALO CALVINO

Bears are made of the same dust as we, and breathe the same winds and drink of the same waters. A bear's days are warmed by the same sun, his dwellings are overdomed by the same blue sky, and his life turns and ebbs with heart-pulsings like ours, and was poured from the same First Fountain. And whether he at last goes to our stingy heaven or no, he has terrestrial immortality. His life not long, not short, knows no beginning, no ending. To him life unstinted, unplanned, is above the accidents of time, and his years, markless and boundless, equal Eternity.

God bless Yosemite bears!

—JOHN MUIR

Watching the animals come and go, and feeling the land swell up to meet them and then feeling it grow still at their departure, I came to think of the migrations as breath, as the land breathing. In spring a great inhalation of light and animals. The long-bated breath of summer. And an exhalation that propelled them all south in the fall.

—BARRY LOPEZ

You can't be suspicious of a tree, or accuse a bird or a squirrel of subversion or challenge the ideology of a violet.

—HAL BORLAND

But if we stop loving animals, aren't we bound to stop loving humans too?

—ALEKSANDR SOLZHENITSYN

If you talk to the animals they will talk with you and you will know each other. If you do not talk to them you will not know them, and what you do not know you will fear. What one fears one destroys.

— CHIEF DAN GEORGE

I have been studying the traits and dispositions of the "lower animals" (so called) and contrasting them with the traits and dispositions of man. I find the result humiliating to me.

— MARK TWAIN

I never saw a wild thing
Sorry for itself.
A small bird will drop dead
From a bough
Without ever having felt sorry for itself.

— D. H. LAWRENCE

I think I could turn and live with animals,
  they are so placid and self-contained;
I stand and look at them long and long.
They do not sweat and whine about their
  condition;
They do not lie awake in the dark and weep
  for their sins;
They do not make me sick discussing their
  duty to God;
Not one is dissatisfied—not one is demented
  with the mania of owning things;
Not one kneels to another, nor to his kind
  that lived thousands of years ago;
Not one is respectable or industrious over the
  whole earth.

—WALT WHITMAN

Animals have these advantages over man: they never hear the clock strike, they die without any idea of death, they have no theologians to instruct them, their last moments are not disturbed by unwelcome and unpleasant ceremonies, their funerals cost them nothing, and no one starts lawsuits over their wills.

—VOLTAIRE

When we lack the society of our fellow men, we take refuge in that of animals, without always losing by the change.

—JEAN HENRI FABRE

Today more than ever before life must be characterized by a sense of Universal responsibility, not only nation to nation and human to human, but also human to other forms of life.

—DALAI LAMA (TENZIN GYATSO)

☾ cycles

One generation passeth away, and another generation cometh: but the earth abideth for ever.

—BIBLE, *ECCLESIASTES* 1:4

But that which has been born of earth
To earth returns;
And that which sprouted from ethereal seed
To heaven's vault goes back.
So nothing dies of all that into being comes,
But each from each is parted
And so takes another form.

—EURIPIDES

Earth knows no desolation. She smells regeneration in the moist breath of decay.

—GEORGE MEREDITH

The Creation is never over. It had a beginning but it has no ending. Creation is always busy making new scenes, new things, and new Worlds.

— IMMANUEL KANT

Creation is not an act but a process; it did not happen five or six thousand years ago but is going on before our eyes. Man is not compelled to be a mere spectator; he may become an assistant, a collaborator, a partner in the process of creation.

— THEODOSIUS DOBZHANSKY

If men could only disintegrate like autumn leaves, fret away, dropping their substance like chlorophyll, would not our attitude towards death be different? Suppose we saw ourselves burning like maples in a golden autumn.

— LOREN EISELEY

Behold this compost! behold it well!
Perhaps every mite has once form'd part of a
sick person—yet behold!
The grass of spring covers the prairies,
The bean bursts noiselessly through the
mould. . . .
Out of its hill rises the yellow maize-stalk,
the lilacs bloom in the dooryards,
The summer growth is innocent and
disdainful above all those strata of sour
dead.

—WALT WHITMAN

M an is the only animal that
contemplates death, and also the only animal
that shows any sign of doubt of its finality.

—WILLIAM E. HOCKING

F lowers and buds fall, and the old and
ripe fall.

—MALAY PROVERB

If you know not how to die, never
trouble yourself; Nature will in a moment fully
and sufficiently instruct you; she will exactly do
that business for you; take you no care for it.

— MICHEL DE MONTAIGNE

In nature, there is less death and
destruction than death and transmutation.

— EDWIN WAY TEALE

The body of man inclines towards the soil
leaving behind his unfulfilled love;
like a stone statue touched by time,
he falls naked on the rich
breast which softens him little by little.

— GEORGE SEFERIS

❨ definitions

Nature is the art of God.

—DANTE ALIGHIERI

Nature is a hanging judge.

—ANONYMOUS

There is no birth in mortal things, and no end in ruinous death. There is only mingling and interchange of parts, and it is this that we call "nature."

—EMPEDOCLES

Nature . . . is a great organ, on which our Lord God plays, and the Devil blows the bellows.

—JOHANN WOLFGANG VON GOETHE

Nature is not anthropomorphic.

—LAO TSU

Nature means the sum of all
phenomena, together with the causes which
produce them; including not only all that
happens, but all that is capable of happening.

—JOHN STUART MILL

[Nature is] a structure of evolving
processes. The reality is the process.

—ALFRED NORTH WHITEHEAD

Nature is a mutable cloud which is
always and never the same.

—RALPH WALDO EMERSON

Nature is what she is—amoral and persistent.

—STEPHEN JAY GOULD

*Nature, it seems, is the popular name
for milliards and milliards and milliards
of particles playing their infinite game
of billiards and billiards and billiards.*

—PIET HEIN

Nature is not a pretty, manicured place maintained for human beings. It is a dynamic continuum, often a violent one.

—DAVE FOREMAN

☾ dominance

And let them have dominion over the fish of the sea, and over the fowl of the air, and over the cattle, and over all the earth, and over every creeping thing that creepeth upon the earth.

—BIBLE, *GENESIS* 1:26

And the fear of you and the dread of you shall be upon every beast of the earth, and upon every fowl of the air, upon all that moveth upon the earth, and upon all the fishes of the sea; into your hand are they delivered.

—BIBLE, *GENESIS* 9:2

It is not really necessary to destroy nature in order to gain God's favor or even his undivided attention.

—IAN MCHARG

For the purpose of attaining freedom in the world of nature, man must use natural science to understand, conquer and change nature and thus attain freedom from nature.

—MAO ZEDONG

The "control of nature" is a phrase conceived in arrogance, born of the Neanderthal age of biology and the convenience of man.

—RACHEL CARSON

. . . We shall continue to have a worsening ecologic crisis until we reject the Christian axiom that nature has no reason for existence save to serve man.

—LYNN WHITE

It was through the Second World War that most of us suddenly appreciated for the first time the power of man's concentrated efforts to understand and control the forces of nature. We were appalled by what we saw.

— VANNEVAR BUSH

Modern man does not experience himself as a part of nature, but as an outside force destined to dominate and conquer. He even talks of a battle with nature, forgetting that if he won the battle he would find himself on the losing side.

— E. F. SCHUMACHER

You could cover the whole world with asphalt, but sooner or later green grass would break through.

— ILYA EHRENBURG

☾ earth

Water rises in mist, freezes into hail, swells in waves, falls headlong in torrents; air becomes thick with clouds and rages with storms; but earth is kind and gentle and indulgent, ever a handmaid in the service of mortals, producing under our compulsion, or lavishing of her own accord, what scents and savours, what juices, what surfaces for the touch, what colours! how honestly she repays the interest lent her!

—PLINY THE ELDER

I demonstrate by means of philosophy that the earth is round, and is inhabited on all sides; that it is insignificantly small, and is borne through the stars.

—JOHANNES KEPLER

I am a passenger on the spaceship Earth.

—R. BUCKMINSTER FULLER

A tiny raft in the enormous, empty night.

—ARCHIBALD MACLEISH

We have today the knowledge and the tools to look at the whole earth, to look at everybody on it, to look at its resources, to look at the state of our technology, and to begin to deal with the whole problem. I think that the tenderness that lies in seeing the earth as small and lonely and blue is probably one of the most valuable things that we have now.

—MARGARET MEAD

There is nothing inorganic. . . . The earth is not a mere fragment of dead history, stratum upon stratum, like the leaves of a book, to be studied by geologists and antiquaries chiefly, but living poetry like the leaves of a tree, which precede flowers and fruit; not a fossil earth but a living earth . . .

— HENRY DAVID THOREAU

We are not aliens but rather like children, barely beginning here and now in the childhood of the race to discover the marvel, the magic, the mystery of this sweet planet that is our inheritance.

— EDWARD ABBEY

Many historical events, hitherto
explained solely in terms of human enterprise,
were actually biotic interactions between people
and land. The characteristics of the land
determined the facts quite as potently as the
characteristics of the men who lived on it.

—ALDO LEOPOLD

Mother Earth, lately called Gaia, is no
more than the commonality of organisms and
the physical environment they maintain with
each passing moment, an environment that will
destabilize and turn lethal if the organisms are
disturbed too much.

—EDWARD O. WILSON

One thing we know for sure. The earth
was not made for man; man was made for the
earth.

—CHIEF SEATTLE

Of all celestial bodies within reach or view . . . the most wonderful and marvelous and mysterious is turning out to be our own planet earth. It is the strangest of all places and there is everything in the world to learn about it. It can keep us awake and jubilant with questions for millennia ahead, if we can learn not to meddle and not to destroy.

—LEWIS THOMAS

Having sampled two
oceans as well as continents, I feel that I know
what the globe itself must feel: there's
nowhere to go.
Elsewhere is nothing more than a far-flung
strew of stars,
burning away.

—JOSEPH BRODSKY

❮ ecology

The Four Laws of Ecology . . .
1. Everything is connected to everything else,
2. Everything must go somewhere,
3. Nature knows best,
4. There is no such thing as a free lunch.

— BARRY COMMONER

The term ecology comes from the Greek word *oikos*, and means "the household." Ecological responsibility, then, begins at home and expands to fill the entire planet.

—JEREMY RIFKIN

Ecology is destined to become the lore of Round River, a belated attempt to convert our collective knowledge of biotic materials into a collective wisdom of biotic navigation. This, in the last analysis, is conservation. . . . Instead of learning more and more about less and less, we must learn more and more about the whole biotic landscape.

—ALDO LEOPOLD

Modern ecological studies leave no doubt that almost any disturbances of natural conditions are likely to have a large variety of indirect unfavorable effects because all components of nature are interrelated and interdependent.

—RENÉ DUBOS

Familiarity with basic ecology will permanently change your world view. You will never again regard plants, microorganisms, and animals (including people) as isolated entities. Instead you will see them—more accurately—as parts of a vast complex of natural machinery— as, in the dictionary definition, "related elements in a system that operates in a definable manner."

—PAUL EHRLICH

The temperature and rainfall are no longer to be entirely the work of some separate, uncivilizable force, but instead in part a product of our habits, our economies, our ways of life.

—BILL MCKIBBEN

Every habitat, from Brazilian rain forest to Antarctic bay to thermal vent, harbors a unique combination of plants and animals. Each kind of plant and animal living there is linked in the food web to only a small part of the other species. Eliminate one species, and another increases in number to take its place. Eliminate a great many species, and the local ecosystem starts to decay visibly. Productivity drops as the channels of the nutrient cycles are clogged. More of the biomass is sequestered in the form of dead vegetation and slowly metabolizing, oxygen-starved mud, or is simply washed away. Less competent pollinators take over as the best-adapted bees, moths, birds, bats, and other specialists drop out. Fewer seeds fall, fewer seedlings sprout. Herbivores decline, and their predators die away in close concert.

—EDWARD O. WILSON

We consider species to be like a brick in the foundation of a building. You can probably lose one or two or a dozen bricks and still have a standing house. But by the time you've lost 20 per cent of species, you're going to destabilize the entire structure. That's the way ecosystems work.

—DONALD A. FALK

Ecology is boring for the same reason that destruction is fun.

—DON DELILLO

❦ economics

Ill fares the land, to hastening ills a prey,
Where wealth accumulates, and men decay.

—OLIVER GOLDSMITH

Earth provides enough to satisfy every
man's need, but not every man's greed.

—MOHANDAS GANDHI

The roots of the problem of
environmental degradation lie in Western
culture's philosophy about nature. . . . The
dominant thinking in the West was articulated
three centuries ago when philosophers
postulated that human behavior focusing
exclusively on the accumulation of money was
somehow sane and rational.

—RICK HILL

Because we depend on so many detailed and subtle aspects of the environment, *any* change imposed on it for the sake of some economic benefit has a price. . . . Sooner or later, wittingly or unwittingly, we must pay for every intrusion on the natural environment.

— BARRY COMMONER

The aim should be to obtain the maximum of well-being with the minimum of consumption. The cultivation and expansion of needs is the antithesis of wisdom.

— E. F. SCHUMACHER

A healthy ecology is the basis for a healthy economy.

— CLAUDINE SCHNEIDER

We abuse land because we regard it as a commodity belonging to us. When we see land as a community to which we belong, we may begin to use it with love and respect. There is no other way for land to survive the impact of mechanized man, nor for us to reap from it the esthetic harvest it is capable, under science, of contributing to culture.

—ALDO LEOPOLD

The more we look at it the more it is apparent that economic growth is a device for providing us with the superfluous at the cost of the indispensable.

—EDWARD GOLDSMITH

It seems to me that the earth may be borrowed but not bought. It may be used but not owned. It gives in response to love and tending, offers its seasonal flowering and fruiting. But we are tenants and not possessors, lovers and not masters. Cross Creek belongs to the wind and the rain, to the sun and the seasons . . . and beyond all, to time.

—MARJORIE KINNON RAWLINGS

"Eternal Progress" is a nonsensical myth. What must be implemented is not a "steadily expanding economy," but a *zero growth economy*, a stable economy. *Economic growth is not only unnecessary but ruinous.*

—ALEKSANDR SOLZHENITSYN

Growth for the sake of growth is the ideology of the cancer cell. Cancer has no purpose but growth; but it does have another result—the death of the host.

— EDWARD ABBEY

And so when we examine the principle of efficiency as we now practice it, we see that it is not really efficiency at all. As we use the word, efficiency means no such thing, or it means short-term or temporary efficiency; which is a contradiction in terms. It means hurrying to nowhere. It means the profligate waste of humanity and nature. It means the greatest profit to the greatest liar. What we have called efficiency has produced among us, and to our incalculable cost, such unprecedented monuments of destructiveness and waste as the strip-mining industry, the Pentagon, the federal bureaucracy, and the family car.

— WENDELL BERRY

❰ extinctions

The beauty and genius of a work of art may be reconceived, though its first material expression be destroyed; a vanished harmony may yet again inspire the composer; but when the last individual of a race of living things breathes no more, another heaven and another earth must pass before such a one can be again.

—CHARLES WILLIAM BEEBE

It is a century now since Darwin gave us
the first glimpse of the origin of species. We
know now what was unknown to all the
preceding caravans of generations; that man is
only a fellow-voyager with other creatures in
the odyssey of evolution, and that his captaincy
of the adventuring ship conveys the power, but
not necessarily the right, to discard at will
among the crew. We should, in the century since
Darwin, have achieved a sense of community
with living things, and of wonder over the
magnitude and duration of the biotic enterprise.

—ALDO LEOPOLD

*(speaking at the dedication of a monument to the recently
extinct passenger pigeon)*

Species are becoming extinct today before they are known to man. Usually we remain in eternal ignorance of what we have lost. Who on receiving a package would toss it out before looking inside: Yet that is what we are doing with our biological heritage.

—THOMAS LOVEJOY

It's like having astronomy without knowing where the stars are.

—EDWARD O. WILSON

Endangered species are sensitive indicators of how we are treating the planet, and we should be listening carefully to their message.

—DONALD A. FALK

Man is modifying the world so fast and so drastically that most animals cannot adapt to the new conditions. In the Himalaya as elsewhere there is a great dying, one infinitely sadder than the Pleistocene extinctions, for man now has the knowledge and the need to save these remnants of his past.

— GEORGE SCHALLER

The bad news is that a lot of species will have perished by the time the ark's gangplank is lowered.

— MICHAEL SOULE

❨ forests

No site in the forest is without
significance, not a glade, not a thicket that does
not provide analogies to the labyrinth of human
thoughts. Who among those people with a
cultivated spirit, or whose heart has been
wounded, can walk in a forest without the forest
speaking to him?

—HONORÉ DE BALZAC

In the woods a man casts off his years, as
the snake his slough, and at what period soever
of life, is always a child.

—RALPH WALDO EMERSON

Sequoias, kings of their race, growing close together like grass in a meadow, poised their brave domes and spires in the sky three hundred feet above the ferns and lilies that enameled the ground; towering serene through the long centuries, preaching God's forestry fresh from heaven.

—JOHN MUIR

Here, man is no longer the center of the world, only a witness, but a witness who is also a partner in the silent life of nature, bound by secret affinities to the trees.

—DAG HAMMARSKJÖLD

Humanity is cutting down its forests, apparently oblivious to the fact that we may not be able to live without them.

—ISAAC ASIMOV

When I cross those pleasant forests which I have saved from the axe, or hear the rustling of the young trees, which I have set out with my own hands, I feel as if I had had some small share in improving the climate, and that if mankind is happy a thousand years from now I shall have been partly responsible in my small way for their happiness. When I plant a young birch tree and see it budding and swaying in the wind, my heart swells with pride.

—ANTON CHEKHOV

[Forests are] the "lungs" of our land, purifying the air and giving fresh strength to our people.

—FRANKLIN D. ROOSEVELT

❨ fragility

The supreme reality of our time is . . .
the vulnerability of our planet.

—JOHN F. KENNEDY

For the first time in my life, I saw the
horizon as a curved line. It was accentuated by a
thin seam of dark blue light—our atmosphere.
Obviously, this was not the "ocean" of air I had
been told it was so many times in my life. I was
terrified by its fragile appearance.

—ULF MERBOLD, GERMAN ASTRONAUT

The entire reach of the biospheric envelope is less than thirty to forty miles from ocean floor to outer space, a distance that, were it horizontal, could be traversed in under an hour by automobile. It is within this narrow vertical band that living creatures and the earth's geochemical processes interact to sustain each other.

—JEREMY RIFKIN

. . . It is an illusion to think that there is anything fragile about the life of the earth; surely this is the toughest membrane imaginable in the universe, opaque to probability, impermeable to death. We are the delicate part, transient and vulnerable as cilia.

—LEWIS THOMAS

The environment is damned near indestructible. It has survived ice ages, bombardments of cosmic radiation, fluctuations of the sun, reversals of the seasons caused by shifts in the planetary axis, collisions of comets and meteors bearing far more force than man's doomsday arsenals. . . . One aspect of the environment is genuinely delicate, though. Namely, the set of conditions favorable to human beings.

— GREGG EASTERBROOK

❨ the future

We must consider the impact our
decisions will have on the next seven
generations.

— IROQUOIS CONFEDERATION

We have not inherited the world from
our forefathers—we have borrowed it from our
children.

— KASHMIRI PROVERB

All the flowers of all the tomorrows are
in the seeds of today.

— CHINESE PROVERB

I believe that this generation may either be the last to exist or the first to have the vision, the daring and the greatness to say, "I will have nothing to do with the destruction of life; I will play no part in this devastation of the land; I am destined to live and work for peaceful construction for I am morally responsible for the world of today and the generations of tomorrow."

—RICHARD ST. BARBE BAKER

I would feel more optimistic about a bright future for man if he spent less time proving that he can outwit Nature and more time tasting her sweetness and respecting her seniority.

—E. B. WHITE

Man will survive as a species for one reason: He can adapt to the destructive effects of our power-intoxicated technology and of our ungoverned population growth, to the dirt, pollution and noise of a New York or Tokyo. And that is the tragedy. It is not man the ecological crisis threatens to destroy but the quality of human life.

—RENÉ DUBOS

People are inexterminable—like flies and bed bugs. There will always be some that survive in cracks and crevices—that's us.

—ROBERT FROST

We haven't too much time left to ensure that the government of the earth, by the earth, for the earth, shall not perish from the people.

—C. P. SNOW AND PHILIP SNOW

We stand now where two roads diverge. But unlike the roads in Robert Frost's familiar poem, they are not equally fair. The road we have long been traveling is deceptively easy, a smooth superhighway on which we progress at great speed, but at its end lies a disaster. The other fork of the road—the one "less travelled by"—offers our last, our only chance to reach a destination that assures the preservation of our earth.

— RACHAEL CARSON

There may yet be, in the untrammeled tenth of America, enough nature, unsecond-guessed by technological arrogance, to build a good future on.

— DAVID R. BROWER

Our children may save us if they are taught to care properly for the planet; but if not, it may be back to the Ice Age or the caves from where we first emerged. Then we'll have to view the universe above from a cold, dark place. No more jet skis, nuclear weapons, plastic crap, broken pay phones, drugs, cars, waffle irons, or television. Come to think of it, that might not be a bad idea.

—JIMMY BUFFET

Wilderness may temporarily dwindle, but wildness won't go away. A ghost wilderness hovers around the entire planet, the millions of tiny seeds of the original vegetation are hiding in the mud on the foot of an arctic tern, in the dry desert sands, or in the wind. These seeds are each uniquely adapted to a specific soil or circumstance; each has its own little form and fluff, ready to float, freeze, or be swallowed, always preserving the germ. Wilderness will inevitably return, but it will not be as fine a world as the one that was glistening in the early morning of the Holocene. Much life will be lost in the wake of human agency on Earth, that of the 20th and 21st centuries. Much has already been lost.

—GARY SNYDER

❦   gardens

God Almighty first planned a garden;
and indeed it is the purest of human pleasures.

— FRANCIS BACON

But though I am an old man, I am but a
young gardener.

— THOMAS JEFFERSON

I want death to find me planting my
cabbages.

— MICHEL DE MONTAIGNE

People from a planet without flowers
would think we must be mad with joy the whole
time to have the things about us.

— IRIS MURDOCH

The best place to find God is in a
garden. You can dig for him there.

—GEORGE BERNARD SHAW

A flower falls, even though we
love it; and a weed grows, even though we
do not love it.

—DOGEN

What is a weed? A plant whose virtues
have not yet been discovered.

—RALPH WALDO EMERSON

Deep in their roots,
All flowers keep the light.

—THEODORE ROETHKE

Like a gardener, I believe that what goes down must come up.

—LYNWOOD L. GIACOMINI

To own a bit of ground, to scratch it with a hoe, to plant seeds and watch their renewal of life—this is the commonest delight of the race, the most satisfactory thing a man can do.

—CHARLES DUDLEY WARNER

. . . He who cultivates a garden, and brings to perfection flowers and fruits, cultivates and advances at the same time his own nature.

—EZRA WESTON

The garden is a proper place for the soul, where concerns of the soul for beauty, contemplation, quiet, and observance take complete precedence over the busier concerns of daily life.

— THOMAS MOORE

... The idea of a garden—as a place, both real and metaphorical, where nature and culture can be wedded in a way that can benefit both— may be as useful to us today as the idea of wilderness has been in the past.

— MICHAEL POLLAN

(**healing**

To him who in the love of nature holds
Communion with her visible forms, she
    speaks
A various language; for his gayer hours
She has a voice of gladness, and a smile
And eloquence of beauty, and she glides
Into his darker musings, with a mild
And healing sympathy that steals away
Their sharpness, ere he is aware.

—WILLIAM CULLEN BRYANT

Those who contemplate the beauty of the Earth find reserves of strength that will endure as long as life lasts. There is symbolic as well as actual beauty in the migration of birds, the ebb and flow of tides, the folded bud ready for spring. There is something infinitely healing in the repeated refrains of nature—the assurance that dawn comes after the night and spring after the winter.

—RACHEL CARSON

Climb the mountains and get their good tidings. Nature's peace will flow into you as the sunshine into the trees. The winds will blow their freshness into you, and the storms their energy, while cares will drop off like autumn leaves.

—JOHN MUIR

Three months of camp life on Lake Tahoe would restore an Egyptian mummy to his pristine vigor, and give him an appetite like an alligator. I do not mean the oldest and driest mummies, of course, but the fresher ones.

— MARK TWAIN

If you are bored, strained, lacerated, enervated by the way we live now, I suggest a night walk as far as you can get from a trace of civilization. This form of walking is a dance, and the ghost that follows you, your moon-cast shadow, is your true androgynous parent, bearing within its distinct outline the child who has always directed your every move.

—JIM HARRISON

Today we look for healing and renewal in the offices of physicians and therapists, when we could be out looking for holy wells and enchanted groves that fortify the soul with their natural mysteries.

— THOMAS MOORE

☾   the heavens

The heavens declare the glory of God;
and the firmament showeth his handiwork.

—BIBLE, *PSALMS* 19:1

The sky is the daily bread of the eyes.

—RALPH WALDO EMERSON

Who knows whither the clouds have fled?
In the unscarred heaven they leave no wake;
And the eyes forget the tears they have shed,
The heart forgets its sorrow and ache.

—JAMES RUSSELL LOWELL

Give me the splendid silent sun with all
his beams full-dazzling.

—WALT WHITMAN

To see the Summer Sky
Is Poetry, though never in a Book it lie—
True poems flee—

—EMILY DICKINSON

Overhead the sanctities of the stars shine forevermore . . . pouring satire on the pompous business of the day which they close, and making the generations of men show slight and evanescent.

—RALPH WALDO EMERSON

These earthly godfathers of Heaven's lights,
That give a name to every fixed star,
Have no more profit of their shining nights
Than those that walk and wot not what
they are.

—WILLIAM SHAKESPEARE

Now the bright morning star, day's
  harbinger,
Comes dancing from the east.

—JOHN MILTON

I try to forget what happiness was,
and when that don't work, I study the stars.

—DEREK WALCOTT

☾ home ground

God gives all men all earth to love,
But since man's heart is small,
Ordains for each one spot shall prove
Belovèd over all.

—RUDYARD KIPLING

I know every stream and every wood between the Rio Grande and the Arkansas. I have hunted and lived over that country. I lived like my fathers before me, and like them, I lived happily.

—TEN BEARS, YAMPARETHDA COMANCHE CHIEF

A man dwells in his native valley like a corolla in its calyx, like an acorn in its cup. *Here*, of course, is all that you love, all that you expect, all that you are. Here is your bride elect, as close to you as she can be got. . . . Bear her away then! Foolish people imagine that what they imagine is somewhere else. That stuff is not made in any factory but their own.

—HENRY DAVID THOREAU

I don't know what Nature is: I sing it.
I live on a hilltop
In a solitary whitewashed cabin.
And that's my definition.

—FERNANDO PESSOA

As time went by, I realized that the particular place I'd chosen was less important than the fact that I'd chosen a place and focused my life around it. . . . What makes a place special is the way it buries itself inside the heart, not whether it's flat or rugged, rich or austere, wet or arid, gentle or harsh, warm or cold, wild or tame. Every place, like every person, is elevated by the love and respect shown toward it, and by the way in which its bounty is received.

—RICHARD K. NELSON

❝ homo sapiens

Man, when perfected, is the best of animals, but, when separated from law and justice, he is the worst of all.

—ARISTOTLE

We must, however, acknowledge, as it seems to me, that man with all his noble qualities . . . still bears in his bodily frame the indelible stamp of his lowly origin.

—CHARLES DARWIN

(his last words)

A human is not a fallen god, but a promoted reptile.

—J. HOWARD MOORE

Man's destiny is to be the sole agent for future evolution of this planet. He is the highest dominant type to be produced over two and a half billion years of the slow biological movement effected by the blind opportunistic workings of natural selection.

—JULIAN HUXLEY

We drink without thirst and we make love anytime, madame; only this distinguishes us from the other animals.

—PIERRE BEAUMARCHAIS

We don't cut our nails to disarm ourselves, Maurizio. On the contrary: just to make us look more civilized, so we can hold our own in a far more desperate struggle than the one our ancestors fought with nothing but their claws.

—LUIGI PIRANDELLO

Man is the only animal which esteems itself rich in proportion to the number and voracity of its parasites.

— GEORGE BERNARD SHAW

You start out as a single cell derived from the coupling of a sperm and an egg, this divides into two, then four, then eight, and so on, and at a certain stage there emerges a single cell which will have as all its progeny the human brain. The mere existence of that cell should be one of the great astonishments of the earth.

— LEWIS THOMAS

The noblest work of God? Man.
Who found it out? Man.

— MARK TWAIN

Man is only a reed, the weakest thing in nature, but he is a thinking reed.

— BLAISE PASCAL

The emergence of intelligence, I am convinced, tends to unbalance the ecology. In other words, intelligence is the great polluter. It is not until a creature begins to manage its environment that nature is thrown into disorder.

— CLIFFORD D. SIMAK

Other animals simply adapt to their environment. Our intelligence seems to have out-paced our sense of place in the universe, and the result is that we're enormously dangerous.

— PETER MATTHIESSEN

Cogito ergo boom.

— SUSAN SONTAG

Man is the only animal whose desires increase as they are fed; the only animal that is never satisfied.

— HENRY GEORGE

Til now man has been up against Nature; from now on he will be up against his own nature.

— DENNIS GABOR

We are the offspring of history and must establish our own paths in this most diverse and interesting of conceivable universes—one indifferent to our suffering, and therefore offering us maximal freedom to thrive, or to fail, in our own chosen way.

— STEPHEN JAY GOULD

Man is the only animal that laughs and weeps; for he is the only animal that is struck by the difference between what things are and what they might have been.

—WILLIAM HAZLITT

I believe I've found the missing link between animal and civilized man. It is us.

—KONRAD LORENZ

That man is an aggressive creature will hardly be disputed. With the exception of certain rodents, no other vertebrate habitually destroys members of its own species.

—ANTHONY STORR

Any species capable of producing, at
this earliest, juvenile stage of its development—
almost instantly after emerging on the earth by
any evolutionary standard—the music of Johann
Sebastian Bach, cannot be all bad.

—LEWIS THOMAS

(hope

I suggest that as biological knowledge grows the ethic will shift fundamentally so that everywhere, for reasons that have to do with the very fiber of the brain, the fauna and flora of a country will be thought part of the national heritage as important as its art, its language, and that astonishing blend of achievement and farce that has always defined our species.

— EDWARD O. WILSON

Out of our human needs, perhaps, will come the strongest argument for preventing the blind destruction of the plant world and its natural habitats. This will not simply be for utilitarian reasons but increasingly because of the demand for that natural solace which the green world and unspoiled scenery provide.

— ANTHONY HUXLEY

Conservation is a bird that flies faster than the shot we aim at it.

—ALDO LEOPOLD

Our earth is but a small star in the great universe. Yet of it we can make, if we choose, a planet unvexed by war, untroubled by hunger or fear, undivided by senseless distinctions of race, color or theory.

—STEPHEN VINCENT BENÉT

It is quite obvious that the human race has made a queer mess of life on this planet. But as a people we probably harbor seeds of goodness that have lain for a long time waiting to sprout when the conditions are right. Man's curiosity, his relentlessness, his inventiveness, his ingenuity have led him into deep trouble. We can only hope that these traits will enable him to claw his way out.

—E. B. WHITE

☾ humility

Where were you when I laid the foundations of the earth? Tell me, if you have understanding.

—BIBLE, *JOB* 38:3

How fleeting are the wishes and efforts of man! how short his time! and consequently how poor will be his results, compared with those accumulated by Nature during whole geological periods! Can we wonder, then, that Nature's productions should be far "truer" in character than man's productions; that they should be infinitely better adapted to the most complex conditions of life, and should plainly bear the stamp of far higher workmanship?

—CHARLES DARWIN

It is the contributions and activities of the plants, bacteria, algae, and the protozoans that carry weight. We vertebrates are the silverfish and cockroaches of this great house, living marginally, in the interstices, profiting from a structure built for and maintained by a different order of being.

—FRED HAPGOOD

There is no need for man and no demand for man, in nature; it is complete without him.

—WILLIAM GRAHAM SUMNER

Let me enjoy the earth no less
Because the all-enacting Might
That fashioned forth its loveliness
Had other aims than my delight.

—THOMAS HARDY

Our concept of the individual is totally warped. All of us are walking communities of microbes. Plants are sedentary communities. Every plant and animal on Earth today is a symbiont, living in close contact with others.

— LYNN MARGULIS

Who are we? We find that we live on an insignificant planet of a humdrum star lost in a galaxy tucked away in some forgotten corner of a universe in which there are far more galaxies than people.

— CARL SAGAN

The destruction of this planet would have no significance on a cosmic scale. To an observer in the Andromeda nebula, the sign of our extinction would be no more than a match flaring for a second in the heavens.

— STANLEY KUBRICK

The world is *not* to be put in order, the world *is* order incarnate. It is for us to put ourselves in unison with this order.

— HENRY MILLER

Out there in the Milky Way and the world without end Amen, America was a tiny speck of a country, a nickel tossed into the Grand Canyon, and American culture the amount of the Pacific Ocean you bring home in your swimsuit.

— GARRISON KEILLOR

For in fact what is man in nature? A Nothing in comparison with the Infinite, and All in comparison with Nothing, a mean between nothing and everything.

— BLAISE PASCAL

I know not what I may appear to the world, but to myself I seem to have been only like a boy playing on the sea-shore, and diverting myself in now and then finding a smoother pebble or a prettier shell than ordinary, whilst the great ocean of truth lay all undiscovered before me.

—ISAAC NEWTON

The world began without man, and it will complete itself without him.

—CLAUDE LEVI-STRAUSS

. . . Rapport with the marvelously purposeless world of nature gives us new eyes for ourselves—eyes in which our very self-importance is not condemned, but seen as something quite other than what it imagines itself to be. In this light all the weirdly abstract and pompous pursuits of men are suddenly transformed into natural marvels of the same order as the immense beaks of the toucans and hornbills, the fabulous tails of the birds of paradise, the towering necks of the giraffes, and the vividly polychromed posteriors of the baboons. Seen thus . . . the self-importance of man dissolves in laughter.

—ALAN WATTS

The more we realize our minuteness and our impotence in the face of cosmic forces, the more astonishing becomes what human beings have achieved.

—BERTRAND RUSSELL

We are none of us good enough for the world we have.

—EDWARD ABBEY

O the great stars.
The rising and the going down. How still.
As though I were not. Am I part of it?

—RAINER MARIA RILKE

If we were to vanish today, the land environment would return to the fertile balance that existed before the human population explosion. But if the ants were to disappear, tens of thousands of other plant and animal species would perish also, simplifying and weakening the land ecosystem almost everywhere.

—EDWARD O. WILSON

Nor is it a new thing for man to invent an existence that he imagines to be above the rest of life; this has been his most consistent intellectual exertion down the millennia. As illusion, it has never worked out to his satisfaction in the past, any more than it does today. Man is embedded in nature.

—LEWIS THOMAS

❮ humor

So, naturalists observe, a flea
Hath smaller fleas that on him prey;
And these have smaller fleas to bite 'em
and so proceed ad infinitum.

—JONATHAN SWIFT

A nature lover is a person who, when treed by a bear, enjoys the view.

—ANONYMOUS

Man is one of the toughest of animated creatures. Only the anthrax bacillus can stand so unfavourable an environment for so long a time.

—H. L. MENCKEN

[When asked what his knowledge of biology had taught him about God, the eminent biologist J. B. S. Haldane replied:]

[He has] an inordinate fondness for beetles.

—J. B. S. HALDANE

Now, my own suspicion is that the universe is not only queerer than we suppose, but queerer than we *can* suppose.

—J. B. S. HALDANE

Oh Lord, help me to be the person my dog thinks I am.

—ANONYMOUS

The English country gentleman galloping after a fox—the unspeakable in full pursuit of the uneatable.

—OSCAR WILDE

I think that I shall never see
A billboard lovely as a tree.
Indeed, unless the billboards fall
I'll never see a tree at all.

— OGDEN NASH

The environment is everything that isn't me.

— ALBERT EINSTEIN

The outdoors is what you have to get through on the way from your apartment into a taxicab.

— FRAN LEBOWITZ

Ants are so much like human beings as to be an embarrassment. They farm fungi, raise aphids as livestock, launch armies into war, use chemical sprays to alarm and confuse enemies, capture slaves, engage in child labor, exchange information ceaselessly. They do everything but watch television.

—LEWIS THOMAS

I'll admit I still get a tiny bit depressed when I try to think about it from her [the Earth's] point of view. Imagine spending four billion years stocking the oceans with seafood, filling the ground with fossil fuels, and drilling the bees in honey production—only to produce a race of bed-wetters!

—BARBARA EHRENREICH

☾ influence

For what has made the sage or poet write
But the fair paradise of Nature's light?

—JOHN KEATS

I know of no subject more elevating, more amazing, more ready to the poetical enthusiasm, the philosophical reflection, and the moral sentiment than the works of nature. Where can we meet such variety, such beauty, such magnificence?

—JAMES THOMSON

It is the marriage of the soul with Nature that makes the intellect fruitful, and gives birth to imagination.

—HENRY DAVID THOREAU

Now I see the secret of the making of the best
persons. It is to grow in the open air, and
to eat and sleep with the earth.

—WALT WHITMAN

Take long walks in stormy weather or
through deep snows in the fields and woods, if
you would keep your spirits up. Deal with brute
nature. Be cold and hungry and weary.

—HENRY DAVID THOREAU

The expansiveness of heaven and earth which is always replete before us is a source of great joy—the light of the sun and moon; the continual return of the four seasons; the beauty of various landscapes; the changes from dawn to dusk in clouds and mists; the appearance of the mountains; the flow of the streams; the rustling of the wind; the moisture of the rain and dew; the purity of the snow; the array of flowers; the growth of fresh grass; the flourishing of trees; the diverse life of birds, animals, fish and insects. If we constantly appreciate this varied beauty of creation, our spirit of harmony will be ceaseless by expanding our mind-and-heart, purifying our emotions, cultivating a moral sense, enkindling joy, and washing away all regrets from our heart.

—KAIBARA EKKEN

After all anybody is as their land and air is. Anybody is as the sky is low or high, the air heavy or clear and anybody is as there is wind or no wind there. It is that which makes them and the arts they make and the work they do and the way they eat and the way they drink and the way they learn and everything.

—GERTRUDE STEIN

☾   instructor

> *But ask now the beasts,*
> *and they shall teach thee;*
> *and the fowls of the air,*
> *and they shall teach thee;*
> *Or speak to the earth,*
> *and it shall tell thee:*
> *And the fishes of the sea*
> *shall declare unto thee.*
>
> —BIBLE, *JOB* 12:7-8

Never does Nature say one thing and Wisdom another.

> —JUVENAL

True wisdom consists in not departing from nature and in molding our conduct according to her laws and model.

> —SENECA

What I know of the divine science and Holy Scripture I learnt in woods and fields.

— ST. BERNARD

Gie me ae spark o' Nature's fire
That's a' the learning I desire.

— ROBERT BURNS

Nature is a gentle guide, but not more sweet and gentle than prudent and just.

— MICHEL DE MONTAIGNE

A certain Philosopher asked St. Anthony: "Father, how can you be so happy when you are deprived of the consolation of books?" Anthony replied: "My book, O philosopher, is the nature of created things, and any time I want to read the words of God, the book is before me."

— THOMAS MERTON

Sweet are the uses of adversity;
Which, like the toad, ugly and venemous,
Wears yet a precious jewel in its head:
And this our life, exempt from public haunt,
Finds tongues in trees, books in the running
*   brooks,*
Sermons in stones, and good in everything.

—WILLIAM SHAKESPEARE

Nature teaches more than she preaches. There are no sermons in stones. It is easier to get a spark out of a stone than a moral.

—JOHN BURROUGHS

Nature's instructions are always slow, those of men are generally premature.

—JEAN-JACQUES ROUSSEAU

It were happy if we studied nature more in natural things, and acted according to nature, whose rules are few, plain, and most reasonable.

—WILLIAM PENN

I went to the woods because I wished to live deliberately, to front only the essential facts of life, and see if I could not learn what it had to teach, and not, when I came to die, discover that I had not lived.

—HENRY DAVID THOREAU

One impulse from a vernal wood
May teach you more of man,
Of moral evil and of good,
Than all the sages can.

—WILLIAM WORDSWORTH

Come forth into the light of things,
Let Nature be your teacher.

—WILLIAM WORDSWORTH

Nature has no instructions for mankind except that our poor beleaguered humanist-democratic way of life, our fantasies of the individual's high worth, our sense that the weak, no less than the strong, have a right to survive, are absurd.

—JOYCE CAROL OATES

❪ kinship

Thou shalt be in league with the stones of the field; and the beasts of the field shall be at peace with thee.

—BIBLE, *JOB* 5:23

Heaven is my father and earth is my mother and even such a small creature as I finds an intimate place in its midst. That which extends throughout the universe, I regard as my body and that which directs the universe, I regard as my nature. All people are my brothers and sisters and all things are my companions.

—CHANG TSAI

*One touch of nature makes the whole
world kin.*

—WILLIAM SHAKESPEARE

(In the context of Troilus and Cressida *(III, iii), the
speaker, Ulysseus, is referring to* human *nature and its
tendency to conform to majority opinions.)*

*I have learned
To look on nature, not as in the hour
Of thoughtless youth; but hearing oftentimes
The still, sad music of humanity.*

—WILLIAM WORDSWORTH

Of thee, O earth, are my bone and
sinew made; to thee, O sun, am I brother. Here
have I my habitat. I am of thee.

—HENRY DAVID THOREAU

The indescribable innocence and beneficence of Nature—such health, such cheer, they afford forever! and such sympathy have they ever with our race, that all Nature would be affected . . . if any man should ever for a just cause grieve.

—HENRY DAVID THOREAU

I am going to venture that the man who sat on the ground in his tipi meditating on life and its meaning, accepting the kinship of all creatures, and acknowledging unity with the universe of things was infusing into his being the true essence of civilization.

—CHIEF LUTHER STANDING BEAR

If I were to name the three most precious resources of life, I should say, books, friends, and nature. . . . Nature we have always with us, an inexhaustible storehouse of that which moves the heart, appeals to the mind, and fires the imagination—health to the body, a stimulus to the intellect, and joy to the soul.

—JOHN BURROUGHS

The basis of any real morality must be the sense of kinship between all living beings.

—HENRY SALT

He who has known how to love the land has loved eternity.

—STEFAN ZEROMSKI

Man is a thinking reed but his great works are done when he is not calculating and thinking. "Childlikeness" has to be restored with long years of training in the art of self-forgetfulness. When this is attained, man thinks yet he does not think. He thinks like the showers coming down from the sky; he thinks like the waves rolling on the ocean; he thinks like the stars illuminating the nightly heavens; he thinks like the green foliage shooting forth in the relaxing spring breeze. Indeed, he is the showers, the ocean, the stars, the foliage.

—DAISETZ SUZUKI

A human being is part of the whole, called by us the universe. A part limited in time and space. He experiences himself, his thoughts and feelings, as something separate from the rest, a kind of optical delusion of his consciousness. This delusion is a kind of prison for us, restricting us to our personal desires and to affection for a few persons nearest to us. Our task must be to free ourselves from this prison by widening our circle of compassion to embrace all living creatures.

—ALBERT EINSTEIN

It was a morning in early summer. A silver haze shimmered and trembled over the lime trees. The air was laden with their fragrance. The temperature was like a caress. I remember—I need not recall—that I climbed up a tree stump and felt suddenly immersed in Itness. I did not call it by that name. I had no need for words. It and I were one.

—BERNARD BERENSON

We human beings of the developed societies have once more been expelled from a garden—the formal garden of Euro-American humanism and its assumptions of human superiority, priority, uniqueness, and dominance. We have been thrown back into that other garden with all the other animals and fungi and insects, where we can no longer be sure we are so privileged. The walls between "nature" and "culture" begin to crumble as we enter a posthuman era. Darwinian insights force occidental people, often unwillingly, to acknowledge their literal kinship with critters.

—GARY SNYDER

❨　landscapes

We come and go, but the land is always here. And the people who love it and understand it are the people who own it—for a little while.

—WILLA CATHER

No disenchantment follows here,
For nature's inspiration moves
The dream which she herself fulfills;
And he whose heart, like valley warmth,
Steams up with joy at scenes like this
Shall never be forlorn.

—GEORGE MEREDITH

A lake is the landscape's most beautiful and expressive feature. It is earth's eye; looking into which the beholder measures the depth of his own nature. The fluviatile trees next the shore are the slender eyelashes which fringe it, and the wooded hills and cliffs around are its overhanging brows.

—HENRY DAVID THOREAU

The landscapes were like a violin bow that played upon my soul.

—STENDHAL

To make a prairie it takes a clover
      and one bee,—
And revery.
The revery alone will do
If bees are few.

—EMILY DICKINSON

The desert landscape is always at its best in the half-light of dawn or dusk. The sense of distance lacks: a ridge nearby can be a far-off mountain range, each small detail can take on the importance of a major variant on the countryside's repetitious theme. The coming of a day promises a change; it is only when the day has fully arrived that the watcher suspects it is the same day returned once again—the same day he has been living for a long time, over and over, still blindingly bright and untarnished by time.

—PAUL BOWLES

To know one's landscape, to feel in sympathy with it, is often to be at peace with life. When all the world seems wrong and the burdens overwhelming he can look out on the familiar fields and hills or get among them and give way to their beauties of form and color as a resource within himself that will be an ever present power of recuperation.

— RICHARD E. DODGE

There is something about the Himalayas . . . something unseen and unknown, a charm that pervades every hour spent among them, a mystery intriguing and disturbing. Confronted by them, a man loses his grasp of ordinary things, perceiving himself as immortal, an entity capable of outdistancing all change, all decay, all life, all death.

— FRANK SMYTHE

I live not in myself, but I become
Portion of that around me; and to me
High mountains are a feeling, but the hum
Of human cities torture.

—LORD BYRON

[The mountains of Yosemite] had feet set in pine-groves and gay emerald meadows, their brows in the sky; bathed in light, bathed in floods of singing water, while snow-clouds avalanche and the winds shine and surge and wreathe about them as the years go by, as if into these mountain mansions Nature had taken pains to gather her choicest treasures to draw her lovers into close and confiding communion with her.

—JOHN MUIR

Loneliness is an aspect of the land. All things in the plain are isolated; there is no confusion of objects in the eye, but one hill or one tree or one man. To look upon that landscape in the early morning, with the sun at your back, is to lose the sense of proportion. Your imagination comes to life, and this, you think, is where Creation was begun.

—N. SCOTT MOMADAY

The land retains an identity of its own, still deeper and more subtle than we can know. Our obligation toward it then becomes simple: to approach with an uncalculating mind, with an attitude of regard. To try to sense the range and variety of its expression—its weather and colors and animals. To intend from the beginning to preserve some of the mystery within it as a kind of wisdom to be experienced, not questioned. And to be alert for its openings, for that moment when something sacred reveals itself within the mundane, and you know the land knows you are there. . . .

—BARRY LOPEZ

☾ laws

If one way be better than another, that you may be sure is Nature's way.

—ARISTOTLE

Nature resolves everything into its component elements, but annihilates nothing.

—LUCRETIUS

Necessity is the mistress and guardian of Nature. Necessity is the theme and artificer of nature, the bridle, the eternal law.

—LEONARDO DA VINCI

Nature hath no goal though she hath law.

—JOHN DONNE

There is a certain Eternal Law, to wit, Reason, existing in the mind of God and governing the whole universe.

— THOMAS AQUINAS

At high tide fish eat ants; at low tide ants eat fish.

— THAI PROVERB

The question before the human race is, whether the God of nature shall govern the world by his own laws, or whether priests and kings shall rule it by fictitious miracles.

— JOHN ADAMS

We call that against nature which cometh against custom. But there is nothing, whatsoever it be, that is not according to nature.

— MICHEL DE MONTAIGNE

(Or, as Goethe puts it, "The unnatural, that too is natural.")

It is a legal maxim that "the law concerneth not itself with trifles,". . . but in the vocabulary of nature, little and great are terms of comparison only; she knows no trifles, and her laws are as inflexible in dealing with an atom as with a continent or a planet.

— GEORGE PERKINS MARSH

It is interesting to contemplate a tangled bank, clothed with many plants of many kinds, with birds singing on the bushes, with various insects flitting about, and with worms crawling through the damp earth, and to reflect that these elaborately contructed forms, so different from each other, and dependent upon each other in so complex a manner, have all been produced by laws acting around us.

— CHARLES DARWIN

The chess board is the world, the pieces are the phenomena of the universe, the rules of the game are what we call the laws of Nature. The player on the other side is hidden from us. We know that his play is always fair, just, and patient. But also we know, to our cost, that he never overlooks a mistake, or makes the smallest allowance for ignorance.

—THOMAS H. HUXLEY

The Laws of Nature are just, but terrible. There is no weak mercy in them. Cause and consequence are inseparable and inevitable. The elements have no forbearance. The fire burns, the water drowns, the air consumes, the earth buries.

—HENRY WADWORTH LONGFELLOW

In nature there are neither rewards nor punishments—there are consequences.

—ROBERT G. INGERSOLL

We have no right to assume that any physical laws exist, or if they have existed up to now, that they will continue to exist in a similar manner in the future.

—MAX PLANCK

☾ loss

As long as nature is seen as in some way outside us, frontiered and foreign, separate, it is lost both to us and in us.

—JOHN FOWLES

I'm truly sorry man's dominion
Has broken Nature's social union.

—ROBERT BURNS

The world is too much with us; late and soon,
Getting and spending we lay waste our
    powers:
Little we see in Nature that is ours.

—WILLIAM WORDSWORTH

Deviation from nature is deviation from happiness.

— SAMUEL JOHNSON

The world to-day is sick to its thin blood for lack of elemental things, for fire before the hands, for water welling from the earth, for air, for dear earth itself underfoot.

— HENRY BESTON

Most of us have lost that sense of unity of biosphere and humanity which would bind and reassure us all with an affirmation of beauty. Most of us do not today believe that whatever the ups and downs of detail within our limited experience, the larger whole is primarily beautiful.

— GREGORY BATESON

We have forgotten the beast and the flower not in order to remember either ourselves or God, but in order to forget everything except the machine.

—JOSEPH WOOD KRUTCH

Many people live in ugly wastelands, but in the absence of imaginative standards, most of them do not even know it.

—C. WRIGHT MILLS

Is it not likely that when the country was new and men were often alone in the fields and the forest they got a sense of bigness outside themselves that has now in some way been lost. . . . Mystery whispered in the grass, played in the branches of trees overhead, was caught up and blown across the American line in clouds of dust at evening on the prairies . . . I can remember old fellows in my home town speaking feelingly of an evening spent on the big empty plains. It had taken the shrillness out of them. They had learned the trick of quiet. . . .

— SHERWOOD ANDERSON

We may be perfectly sure of where we are in relation to the supermarket and the next coffee break, but I doubt that any of us knows where he is in relation to the stars and to the solstices.

— N. SCOTT MOMADAY

When the Pleiades and the wind in the
grass are no longer a part of the human spirit, a
part of very flesh and bone, man becomes, as it
were, a kind of cosmic outlaw, having neither
the completeness and integrity of the animal nor
the birthright of a true humanity.

— HENRY BESTON

In losing stewardship we lose
fellowship; we become outcasts from the
great neighborhood of creation.

— WENDELL BERRY

Never have people been more the
masters of their environment. Yet never has a
people felt more deceived and disappointed. For
never has a people expected so much more than
the world could offer.

— DANIEL J. BOORSTIN

We told the native peoples of North America that their relationships with the land were worthless, primitive. Now we are a culture that spends millions trying to find this knowledge, trying to reestablish a sense of well-being with the earth.

—BARRY LOPEZ

Now we are no longer primitive; now the whole world seems not-holy. We have drained the light from the boughs in the sacred grove and snuffed it in the high places and along the banks of the sacred streams. We as a people have moved from pantheism to pan-atheism.

—ANNIE DILLARD

Our life, in the age of technology, risks becoming ever more anonymous and a function of the productive process. Man thus becomes incapable of enjoying the beauties of creation, and, even more, of reading in them the reflection of the face of God.

— POPE JOHN PAUL II

I think that the ultimate irony of organic evolution is that in the instant of achieving self-understanding through the mind of man, it doomed its most beautiful creations.

— EDWARD O. WILSON

(remark occasioned by destruction of the Amazonian rain forest)

☾   mystery

In all things of nature there is something of the marvelous.

—ARISTOTLE

I do not know whether I was then a man dreaming I was a butterfly, or whether I am now a butterfly dreaming I am a man.

—CHUANG TSE

In nature's infinite book of secrecy
A little I can read.

—WILLIAM SHAKESPEARE

All know that the drop merges into the ocean, but few know that the ocean merges into the drop.

—KABIR

Love the animals, love the plants, love everything. If you love everything, you will perceive the divine mystery in things. Once you perceive it, you will begin to comprehend it better every day. And you will come at last to love the whole world with an all-embracing love.

—FYODOR DOSTOEVSKY

There is not so contemptible a plant or animal that does not confound the most enlarged understanding.

—JOHN LOCKE

This world, after all our science and sciences, is still a miracle; wonderful, inscrutable, magical and more, to whosoever will think of it.

—THOMAS CARLYLE

The fairest thing we can experience is the mysterious. It is the fundamental emotion which stands at the cradle of true art and true science.

—ALBERT EINSTEIN

All nature is but art, unknown to thee;
All chance, direction, which thou canst
*   not see;*
All discord, harmony not understood;
All partial evil, universal good.

—ALEXANDER POPE

As we acquire more knowledge, things do not become more comprehensible, but more mysterious.

—ALBERT SCHWEITZER

However much you knock at nature's door, she will never answer you in comprehensible words.

—IVAN TURGENEV

The thing that makes the flowers open and the snowflakes fall must contain a wisdom and a final secret as intricate and beautiful as the blooming camellia or the clouds gathering above, so white and pure in the blackness.

—ANNE RICE

I have never asked that nature open any doors to reveal the truth of spirit or mystery; I aspire to no shaman's path; I expect no vision, no miracles except the ones that fill every instant of ordinary life.

—RICHARD K. NELSON

It began in mystery, and it will end in mystery, but what a savage and beautiful country lies between.

—DIANE ACKERMAN

☾ the nature of nature

Nature is not benevolent; with ruthless indifference she makes all things serve their purpose.

—LAO TSU

Though you drive away nature with a pitchfork, she always returns.

—HORACE

Nature is wont to hide herself.
She rests by changing.

—HERACLITUS

Nature does nothing in vain.

—ARISTOTLE

Nature, to be commanded, must be obeyed.

— FRANCIS BACON

Nature is an infinite sphere of which the center is everywhere and the circumference nowhere.

— BLAISE PASCAL

The perpetual admonition of nature to us is, "The world is new, untried. Do not believe the past. I give you the universe a virgin today."

— RALPH WALDO EMERSON

Nature is so uncomfortable. Grass is hard and lumpy and damp, and full of dreadful insects.

— OSCAR WILDE

Nothing is so cruel, so wanton, so unfeeling as nature; she moves with the weight of a glacier carrying everything before her.

— CLARENCE DARROW

Perhaps nature is our best assurance of immortality.

— ELEANOR ROOSEVELT

Into every empty corner, into all forgotten things and nooks, Nature struggles to pour life, pouring life into the dead, life into life itself.

— HENRY BESTON

How cunningly nature hides every wrinkle of her inconceivable antiquity under roses and violets and morning dew!

— RALPH WALDO EMERSON

Nature has neither kernel nor shell; she is everything at once.

— JOHANN WOLFGANG VON GOETHE

The reason for the sublime simplicity in the works of nature lies all too often in the sublime shortsightedness in the observer.

— GEORGE CHRISTOPH LICHTENBERG

And the more we learn of the nature of things, the more evident is it that what we call rest is only unperceived activity; that seeming peace is silent but strenuous battle. In every part, at every moment, the state of the cosmos is the expression of a transitory adjustment of contending forces; a scene of strife, in which all the combatants fall in turn. What is true of each part, is true of the whole.

— THOMAS H. HUXLEY

Men argue, nature acts.

—VOLTAIRE

Nature takes no account of even the most reasonable of human excuses.

—JOSEPH WOOD KRUTCH

There is nothing useless in nature; not even uselessness itself.

—MICHEL DE MONTAIGNE

What nature delivers to us is never stale. Because what nature creates has eternity in it.

—ISAAC BASHEVIS SINGER

Nature cares nothing for logic, our human logic; she has her own, which we do not recognize and do not acknowledge until we are crushed under its wheel.

—IVAN TURGENEV

❨ oceans

All the rivers run into the sea;
yet the sea is not full;
unto the place from whence the rivers come,
thither they return again.

—BIBLE, *ECCLESIASTES* 1:7

The earth and ocean seem
To sleep in one another's arms, and dream
Of waves, flowers, clouds, woods, rocks, and
all that we
Read in their smiles, and call reality.

—PERCY BYSSHE SHELLEY

The seas are the heart's blood of the earth. Plucked up and kneaded by the sun and the moon, the tides are systole and diastole of earth's veins.

—HENRY BESTON

In its mysterious past [the sea] encompasses all the dim origins of life and receives in the end, after, it may be, many transmutations, the dead husks of that same life. For all at last returns to the sea—to Oceanus, the ocean river, like the ever-flowing stream of time, the beginning and the end.

—RACHEL CARSON

The sea never changes and its works, for all the talk of men, are wrapped in mystery.

—JOSEPH CONRAD

There is, one knows not what sweet mystery about this sea, whose gently awful stirrings seem to speak of some hidden soul beneath . . . And meet it is, that over these sea pastures, wide-rolling watery prairies and Potters' Fields of all four continents, the waves should rise and fall, and ebb and flow unceasingly; for here, millions of mixed shades and shadows, drowned dreams, somnambulisms, reveries; all that we call lives and souls, lie dreaming, dreaming, still; tossing like slumberers in their beds; the ever rolling waves but made so by their restlessness.

—HERMAN MELVILLE

« progress

The belief that we can manage the
Earth and improve on Nature is probably the
ultimate expression of human conceit, but it has
deep roots in the past and is almost universal.

—RENÉ DUBOS

Let us not, however, flatter ourselves
overmuch on account of our human conquests
over nature. For each such conquest takes its
revenge on us. Each [has] . . . unforeseen effects
which only too often cancel out the [intended
consequences].

—FRIEDRICH ENGELS

... Twenty centuries of "progress" have brought the average citizen a vote, a national anthem, a Ford, a bank account, and a high opinion of himself, but not the capacity to live in high density without befouling and denuding his environment, nor a conviction that such capacity, rather than such density, is the true test of whether he is civilized.

— ALDO LEOPOLD

Destroying rain forest for economic gain is like burning a Renaissance painting to cook a meal.

— EDWARD O. WILSON

If people destroy something replaceable made by mankind, they are called vandals; if they destroy something irreplaceable made by God, they are called developers.

— JOSEPH WOOD KRUTCH

What have we achieved in mowing down mountain ranges, harnessing the energy of mighty rivers, or moving whole populations about like chess pieces, if we ourselves remain the same restless, miserable, frustrated creatures we were before?

—HENRY MILLER

Progress, under whose feet the grass mourns and the forest turns into paper from which newspaper plants grow, has subordinated the purpose of life to the means of subsistence and turned us into the nuts and bolts for our tools.

—KARL KRAUS

Not blind opposition to progress, but opposition to blind progress.

—SIERRA CLUB MOTTO

❨ religious teachings

Even a wise man acts under the impulse of his nature: all beings follow nature. Of what use is restraint?

—BHAGAVAD GITA

Wonder of wonders! Intrinsically all living beings are Buddhas, endowed with wisdom and virtue, but because men's minds have become inverted through delusive thinking they fail to perceive this.

—BUDDHA

Of all that the Holy One created in His world, He did not create a single thing that is useless.

—TALMUD

The encounter of God and man in nature is thus conceived in Judaism as a seamless web with man as the leader and custodian of the natural world. . . . Man was given dominion over nature, but was commanded to behave towards the rest of creation with justice and compassion. Man lives, always, in tension between his power and the limits set by his conscience.

—ARTHUR HERTZBERG

All you under the heaven! Regard heaven as your father, earth as your mother, and all things as your brothers and sisters.

—THE ORACLE OF ATSUTA (SHINTO)

Unity, trusteeship and accountability, that is tawheed, khalifa and akhrah, the three central concepts of Islam, are also the pillars of the environmental ethics of Islam. They constitute the basic values taught by the Qur'an.

—ABDULLAH OMAR NASEEF

Assuredly the creation of the heavens and the earth is greater than the creation of humankind; yet most people understand not.

—KORAN

The earth will not continue to offer its harvest, except with faithful stewardship. We cannot say we love the land and then take steps to destroy it for use by future generations.

—POPE JOHN PAUL II

As children of heaven and earth, human beings must take heaven and earth as the model for their conduct; heaven and earth have nothing else at heart than to be sympathetic to all things. They have no other purpose or function than to bring forth and nourish all things. Humans also receive this heart and should always aspire to have a heart which is sympathetic and kind to others.

—KAIBARA EKKEN

God and nature and any other agent make what is best in the whole, but not what is best in every single part, except in order to the whole. . . . And the whole itself, which is the universe of creatures, is better and more perfect if some things in it can fail in goodness, and do sometimes fail, God not preventing this.

—THOMAS AQUINAS

We are of the soil and soil is of us. We love the birds and beasts that grew with us on this soil. They drank the same water we did and breathed the same air. We are all one in nature. Believing so, there was in our hearts a great peace and a welling kindness for all living, growing things.

— CHIEF LUTHER STANDING BEAR

Water, air, soil, minerals, energy resources, plants, animal life and space are to be valued and conserved because they are God's creations and not solely because they are useful to human beings.

— BOOK OF DISCIPLINE, UNITED METHODIST CHURCH

❦ rivers

The flow of the river is ceaseless and its water is never the same. The bubbles that float in the pools, now vanishing, now forming, are not of long duration: so in the world are man and his dwellings. . . . [People] die in the morning, they are born in the evening, like foam on the water.

—KAMO CHOMEI

I was born upon thy bank, river,
My blood flows in thy stream,
And thou meanderest forever
At the bottom of my dream.

—HENRY DAVID THOREAU

Since water still flows, though we cut it
with swords
And sorrow returns, though we drown it
with wind,
Since the world can in no way answer to
our craving,
I will loosen my hair tomorrow and take to
a fishing boat.

—LI PO

Living is moving, time is a live creek
bearing changing lights.

—ANNIE DILLARD

I chatter over stony ways
In little sharps and trebles
I bubble over eddying bays
I babble on the pebbles. . . .
And out again I curve and flow
To join the brimming river
For men may come and men may go,
But I go on forever.

—ALFRED, LORD TENNYSON

And an ingenious Spaniard says, that rivers and the inhabitants of the watery element were made for wise men to contemplate, and fools to pass by without consideration.

—ISAAK WALTON

A river seems a magic thing. A magic, moving, living part of the very earth itself.

—LAURA GILPIN

I gave my heart to the mountains the minute I stood beside this river with its spray in my face and watched it thunder into foam, smooth to green glass over sunken rocks, shatter to foam again. I was fascinated by how it sped by and yet was always there; its roar shook both the earth and me.

— WALLACE STEGNER

Running through our civilization, the river's history lies central to local culture, and the tale of each of our rivers must be learned and told to every member of that river's society. . . . Perhaps the river's story can be a starting point in a new regard for all waterways and for the planet. The new attitude must embrace a deeper commitment to the well-being of a place based on its history, on its role in life, and on the security, joy and wonder that we know while living in that corner of the universe.

— TIM PALMER

I sat there and forgot and forgot, until what remained was the river that went by and I who watched. On the river the heat mirages danced with each other and then they danced through each other and then they joined hands and danced around each other. Eventually the watcher joined the river, and there was only one of us. I believe it was the river.

—NORMAN MACLEAN

❲ ruination

The lands wait for those who can discern their rhythms. The peculiar genius of each continent, each river valley, the rugged mountains, the placid lakes, all call for relief from the constant burden of exploitation.

—VINE DELORIA

What now remains compared with what then existed is like the skeleton of a sick man, all the fat and soft earth having been wasted away, and only the bare framework of the land being left.

—PLATO

(on deforestation in Attica)

I durst not laugh for fear of opening my lips and receiving the bad air.

—WILLIAM SHAKESPEARE

Man has been endowed with reason, with the power to create, so that he can add to what he's been given. But up to now he hasn't been a creator, only a destroyer. Forests keep disappearing, rivers dry up, wild life's become extinct, the climate's ruined and the land grows poorer and uglier every day.

—ANTON CHEKHOV

For the first time in the history of the world, every human being is now subjected to contact with dangerous chemicals, from the moment of conception until death.

—RACHAEL CARSON

Industrial vomit . . . fills our skies and seas. Pesticides and herbicides filter into our foods. Twisted automobile carcasses, aluminum cans, non-returnable glass bottles and synthetic plastics form immense kitchen middens in our midst as more and more of our detritus resists decay. We do not even begin to know what to do with our radioactive wastes—whether to pump them into the earth, shoot them into outer space, or pour them into the oceans. Our technological powers increase, but the side effects and potential hazards also escalate.

—ALVIN TOFFLER

We have met the enemy, and it is us.

—WALT KELLY

How can the spirit of the earth like the White man? . . . Everywhere the White man has touched, it is sore.

—WINTU INDIAN

It gets to seem as if way back in the Garden of Eden after the Fall, Adam and Eve had begged the Lord to forgive them and He, in his boundless exasperation, had said, "All right, then, Stay. Stay in the Garden. Get civilized. Procreate. Muck it up." And they did.

—DIANE ARBUS

I am sorry to say that there is too much point to the wisecrack that life is extinct on other planets because their scientists were more advanced than ours.

—JOHN F. KENNEDY

We have forgotten how to be good guests, how to walk lightly on the earth as its other creatures do.

—BARBARA WARD

We presume to change the natural environment for all the living creatures on this earth. Do we, who are transients on this earth, and not overly wise, really believe we have the right to upset the order of nature, an order established by a power higher than man?

—ADMIRAL HYMAN G. RICKOVER

. . . The bulldozer and not the atomic bomb may turn out to be the most destructive invention of the 20th century.

—PHILIP SHABECOFF

We must put the foolishness out of our mind that man is going to destroy the Earth, because man is not that powerful. Man may be stupid enough to destroy his ability to live on the Earth, but man will not destroy the Earth. The Earth will purify itself if it takes a billion years. The Earth has time to do that.

—JOHN TRUDELL

☾ sacred nature

> What else is nature but God?
>
> — SENECA

> I, the fiery life of divine essence, am
> aflame beyond the beauty of the meadows, I
> gleam in the waters, and I burn in the sun,
> moon, and stars . . . I awaken everything to life.
>
> — HILDEGARD OF BINGEN

> Those honor Nature well who teach
> that she can speak on everything, even on
> theology.
>
> — BLAISE PASCAL

The world is charged with the grandeur
of God.
It will flame out, like shining from shook
foil . . .

—GERARD MANLEY HOPKINS

This is what I have learnt from my
contact with the earth—the diaphany of
the divine at the heart of a glowing universe,
the divine radiating from the depths of matter
a-flame.

—PIERRE TEILHARD DE CHARDIN

All are but parts of one stupendous whole.
Whose body nature is, and God the soul.

—ALEXANDER POPE

The quest of man for God, which becomes in the end the most ardent and enthralling of all his quests, begins with the first vague questioning of nature and a sense of something unseen both in himself and her.

—SRI AUROBINDO

And I have felt
A presence that disturbs me with the joy
Of elevated thoughts, a sense sublime
Of something far more deeply interfused,
Whose dwelling is the light of setting suns,
And the round ocean and the living air,
And the blue sky, and in the mind of man:
A motion and a spirit, that impels
All thinking things, all objects of all thought,
And rolls through all things.

—WILLIAM WORDSWORTH

Earth, with her thousand voices, praises God.

—SAMUEL TAYLOR COLERIDGE

All the wilderness seems to be full of tricks and plans to drive and draw us up into God's light.

—JOHN MUIR

Nature is full of genius, full of the divinity; so that not a snowflake escapes its fashioning hand.

—HENRY DAVID THOREAU

Whether you like it or not, whether you know it or not, secretly all nature seeks God and works toward him.

—MEISTER ECKHART

The sky is round, and I have heard that the earth is round like a ball, and so are all the stars. The wind, in its greatest power, whirls. Birds make their nests in circles, for theirs is the same religion as ours. . . . Even the seasons form a great circle in their changing, and always come back again to where they were.

—BLACK ELK

Land is immortal, for it harbors the mysteries of creation.

—ANWAR EL-SADAT

Every walk to the woods is a religious rite, every bath in the stream is a saving ordinance. Communion service is at all hours, and the bread and wine are from the heart and marrow of Mother Earth. The beauty of natural religion is that you have it all the time. . . . It is of today; it is now and here; it is everywhere.

—JOHN BURROUGHS

If, then, I call God nature, it is for greater simplicity, and because it irritates the theologians.

—ANDRÉ GIDE

Every part of this soil is sacred in the estimation of my people. Every hillside, every valley, every plain and grove, has been hallowed by some sad or happy event in the days long vanished. Even the rocks, which seem to be dumb and dead as they swelter in the sun along the silent shore, thrill with memories of stirring events connected with the lives of my people . . .

—CHIEF SEATTLE

I do not think it is important whether a man enters religion by the front door or the back door as long as he enters. . . . If to find God by the garden path is the back door, then by all means go down the garden path.

—LIN YUTANG

I love to think of nature as an unlimited broadcasting station, through which God speaks to us every hour, if we only will tune in.

— GEORGE WASHINGTON CARVER

I believe in God, only I spell it N-a-t-u-r-e.

— FRANK LLOYD WRIGHT

To live we must daily break the body and shed the blood of Creation. When we do this lovingly, knowingly, skillfully, reverently, it is a sacrament. When we do it greedily, clumsily, ignorantly, destructively, it is a desecration. By such desecration we condemn ourselves to spiritual and moral loneliness, and others to want.

— WENDELL BERRY

But it is not in "God's house" that I
feel his presence most—it is in his outdoors, on
some sun-warmed slope of pine needles or by
the surf. It is there that the numbing categories
men have devised to contain this mystery—sin
and redemption and incarnation and so on—
fall away, leaving the overwhelming sense of
the goodness and the sweetness at work in
the world.

—BILL MCKIBBEN

☾   science

Science teaches those who immerse themselves in it to know the workings of God in Nature, but the practice of science does more than this. As the depth of their understanding grows, its students cannot fail to learn the interdependence of all creation. This is even more than the brotherhood of man, this is the harmony of all nature. Furthermore, those who devote themselves to science thereby learn humility.

— MAGNUS PYKE

Man masters nature, not by force but by understanding. This is why science has succeeded were magic failed: because it has looked for no spell to cast over nature.

—JACOB BRONOWSKI

A dream may let us deeper into the secret of nature than a hundred concerted experiments.

— RALPH WALDO EMERSON

Science has, as its whole purpose, the rendering of the physical world understandable and beautiful. Without this you have only tables and statistics. The measure of our success is our ability to live with this knowledge effectively, actively and eventually with delight. If we succeed we will be able to cope with our knowledge and not create despair.

— J. ROBERT OPPENHEIMER

God does not play dice with the universe.

—ALBERT EINSTEIN

God not only plays dice, he also sometimes throws the dice where they cannot be seen.

—STEPHEN HAWKING

The highest wisdom has but one science—the science of the whole—the science explaining the whole creation and man's place in it.

—LEO TOLSTOY

The saddest aspect of life right now is that science gathers knowledge faster than society gathers wisdom.

—ISAAC ASIMOV

The way to solve the conflict between human values and technological needs is not to run away from technology. That's impossible. The way to resolve the conflict is to break down the barriers of dualistic thought that prevent a real understanding of what technology is—not an exploitation of nature, but a fusion of nature and the human spirit into a new kind of creation that transcends both.

—ROBERT PERSIG

In the face of a rational, scientific approach to the land, which is more widely sanctioned, esoteric insights and speculations are frequently overshadowed, and what is lost is profound. The land is like poetry: it is inexplicably coherent, it is transcendent in its meaning, and it has the power to elevate a consideration of human life.

—BARRY LOPEZ

❦ seeing

It is in man's heart that the life
of nature's spectacle exists; to see it, one
must feel it.

—JEAN-JACQUES ROUSSEAU

To the attentive eye, each moment
of the year has its own beauty, and in the same
field, it beholds, every hour, a picture which
was never seen before, and which shall never
be seen again.

—RALPH WALDO EMERSON

Nature will bear the closest inspection.
She invites us to lay our eye level with her
smallest leaf, and take an insect view of it plain.

—HENRY DAVID THOREAU

If we had a keen vision and feeling of all
ordinary human life, it would be like hearing the
grass grow and the squirrel's heart beat, and we
should die of that roar which lies on the other
side of silence. As it is, the quickest of us walk
about well wadded with stupidity.

—GEORGE ELIOT

A child's world is fresh and new and
beautiful, full of wonder and excitement.
It is our misfortune that for most of us that
clear-eyed vision, that true instinct for what
is beautiful and awe-inspiring, is dimmed and
even lost before we reach adulthood.

—RACHEL CARSON

Nobody, living upon the remotest
barren crag in the ocean, could complain of
a dull landscape so long as he would lift his
eyes. In the sky there was a new landscape
every minute, in every pool of the sea rocks,
a new world.

—T. H. WHITE

Look. This is your world! You can't
not look. There is no other world. This is
your world; it is your feast. You inherited this;
you inherited these eyeballs; you inherited
this world of color. Look at the greatness of
the whole thing. Look! Don't hesitate—look!
Open your eyes. Don't blink, and look, look—
look further.

—CHOGYAM TRUNGPA

If only we could pull out our brain and use only our eyes.

— PABLO PICASSO

I think we would be able to live in this world more peaceably if our spirituality were to come from looking not just into infinity but very closely at the world around us—and appreciating its depth and divinity.

— THOMAS MOORE

Each day I live in a glass room
Unless I break it with the thrusting
Of my senses and pass through
The splintered walls to the great landscape.

— MERVYN PEAKE

❨ solace

Nature goes forward in her never-ending course, and cares nothing for the race of man that is ever passing before her. . . . When man turns to reflection and resigns himself to the inevitable . . . then the eternal, unchangeable order of Nature has a comforting and peaceful influence.

—WILHELM VON HUMBOLDT

I remember a hundred lovely lakes, and recall the fragrant breath of pine and fir and cedar and poplar trees. The trail has strung upon it, as upon a thread of silk, opalescent dawns and saffron sunsets. It has given me blessed release from care and worry and the troubled thinking of our modern day . . . Whenever the pressure of our complex city life thins my blood and benumbs my brain, I seek relief in the trail; and when I hear the coyote wailing to the yellow dawn, my cares fall from me—I am happy.

— HAMLIN GARLAND

I experienced sometimes that the most sweet and tender, the most innocent and encouraging society may be found in any natural object, even for the most melancholy man.

— HENRY DAVID THOREAU

The best remedy for those who are afraid, lonely or unhappy is to go outside, somewhere where they can be quiet, alone with the heavens, nature and God. Because only then does one feel that all is as it should be and that God wishes to see people happy, amidst the simple beauty of nature. . . . I firmly believe that nature brings solace in all troubles.

—ANNE FRANK

For the mind disturbed, the still beauty of dawn is nature's finest balm.

—EDWIN WAY TEALE

It was a beautiful day here to-day, with bright, new, wide-opened sunshine, and lovely new scents in the fresh air, as if new blood were rising. And the sea came in great long waves thundering splendidly from the unknown. It is perfect, with a strong, pure wind blowing. What does it matter about that seething scrimmage of mankind in Europe? If that were indeed the only truth, one might indeed despair.

— D. H. LAWRENCE

(entry in journal written during World War 1)

Each of us needs to withdraw from the cares which will not withdraw from us. We need hours of aimless wandering or spates of time sitting on park benches, observing the mysterious world of ants and the canopy of treetops.

— MAYA ANGELOU

☾ solitude

You ask me, "Why dwell among green
    mountains?"
I laugh in silence; my soul is quiet.
Peach blossom follows the moving water;
Here is a heaven and earth, beyond the world
    of men.

—LI PO

How often we forget all time, when lone,
Admiring Nature's universal throne,
Her woods, her wilds, her waters, the intense
Reply of hers to our intelligence.

—LORD BYRON

Away, away, from men and towns,
To the wild wood and the downs,—
To the silent wilderness,
Where the soul need not repress
Its music.

—PERCY BYSSHE SHELLEY

Touch the earth, love the earth, honour
the earth, her plains, her valleys, her hills, and
her seas; rest your spirit in her solitary places.

—HENRY BESTON

I would rather sit on a pumpkin, and have it all to myself, than to be crowded on a velvet cushion.

—HENRY DAVID THOREAU

Only by going alone in silence, without baggage, can one truly get into the heart of the wilderness. All other travel is mere dust and hotels and baggage and chatter.

—JOHN MUIR

Every prophet has to come from civilization, but every prophet has to go into the wilderness. He must have a strong impression of a complex society and all that it has to give, and then he must serve periods of isolation and meditation. This is the process by which psychic dynamite is made.

—WINSTON CHURCHILL

I lived in solitude in the country and
noticed how the monotony of a quiet life
stimulates the creative mind.

—ALBERT EINSTEIN

If you want inner peace find it
in solitude, not speed, and if you would find
yourself, look to the land from which you
came and to which you go.

—STEWART UDALL

In order to understand the world, one
has to turn away from it on occasion; in order to
serve men better, one has to hold them at a
distance for a time. But where can one find the
solitude necessary to vigour, the deep breath in
which the mind collects itself and courage
gauges its strength?

—ALBERT CAMUS

❧ stewardship

It has been my opinion, that he who receives an Estate from his ancestors is under some kind of obligation to transmit the same to their posterity.

—BENJAMIN FRANKLIN

I am I plus my surroundings and if I do not preserve the latter, I do not preserve myself.

—JOSÉ ORTEGA Y GASSET

In democratic societies people may think that their government is bound by an ecological version of the Hippocratic oath, to take no action that knowingly endangers biodiversity. But that is not enough. The commitment must be much deeper—to let no species knowingly die, to take all reasonable action to protect every species and race in perpetuity.

—EDWARD O. WILSON

Clearly the problem of man and nature is not one of providing a decorative background for the human play, or even ameliorating the grim city; it is the necessity of sustaining nature as source of life, milieu, teacher, sanctum, challenge and, most of all, of rediscovering nature's corollary of the unknown in the self, the source of meaning.

—IAN MCHARG

So long as we are under the illusion that we know best what is good for the earth and for ourselves, then we will continue our present course, with its devastating consequences on the entire earth community. Our best procedure might be to consider that we need not a human answer to an earth problem, but an earth answer to an earth problem. The earth will solve its problems, and possibly our own, if we will let the earth function in its own ways. We need only listen to what the earth is telling us.

—THOMAS BERRY

❨ trees

The tree which moves some to tears of joy is in the eyes of others only a green thing that stands in the way. Some see nature all ridicule and deformity . . . and some scarce see nature at all. But to the eyes of the man of imagination, nature is imagination itself.

—WILLIAM BLAKE

He that plants trees loves others beside himself.

—THOMAS FULLER

Here is one of my favorites now before me, a fine yellow poplar, quite straight, perhaps 90 feet high, and four feet thick at the butt. How strong, vital, enduring! how dumbly eloquent! What suggestions of imperturbability and *being*, as against the human trait of mere *seeming*. Then the qualities, almost emotional, palpably artistic, heroic . . . so innocent and harmless, yet so savage. It *is*, yet it says nothing.

— WALT WHITMAN

We all travel the milky way together, trees and men . . . trees are travellers, in the ordinary sense. They make journeys, not very extensive ones, it is true; but our own little comes and goes are only little more than tree-wavings—many of them not so much.

— JOHN MUIR

O chestnut-tree, great-rooted blossomer,
Are you the leaf, the blossom or the bole?
O body swayed to music, O brightening
    glance,
How can we know the dancer from the
    dance?

—WILLIAM BUTLER YEATS

We have nothing to fear and a great
deal to learn from trees, that vigorous and
pacific tribe which without stint produces
strengthening essences for us, soothing balms,
and in whose gracious company we spend so
many cool, silent and intimate hours.

—MARCEL PROUST

Who leaves the pine tree, leaves his friend,
Unnerves his strength, invites his end.

—RALPH WALDO EMERSON

The hemlock's nature thrives on cold;
The gnash of northern winds
Is sweetest nutriment to him,
His best Norwegian wines.

—EMILY DICKINSON

I like trees because they seem more resigned to the way they have to live than other things do.

—WILLA CATHER

Evolution did not intend trees to grow singly. Far more than ourselves they are social creatures, and no more natural as isolated specimens than man is as a marooned sailor or hermit.

—JOHN FOWLES

Except during the nine months before he draws his first breath, no man manages his affairs as well as a tree does.

— GEORGE BERNARD SHAW

Tree at my window, window tree,
My sash is lowered when night comes on;
But let there never be curtain drawn
Between you and me.

— ROBERT FROST

Every year a given tree creates absolutely from scratch ninety-nine percent of its living parts. Water lifting up tree trunks can climb one hundred and fifty feet an hour; in full summer a tree can, and does, heave a ton of water every day. A big elm in a single season might make as many as *six million* leaves, wholly intricate, without budging an inch; I couldn't make one. A tree stands there, accumulating deadwood, mute and rigid as an obelisk, but secretly it seethes; it splits, sucks and stretches; it heaves up tons and hurls them out in a green, fringed fling.

—ANNIE DILLARD

. . . It is not Christ who is crucified now; it is the tree itself, and on the bitter gallows of human greed and stupidity. Only suicidal morons, in a world already choking to death, would destroy the best natural air-conditioner creation affords.

—JOHN FOWLES

Trees are the earth's endless effort to speak to the listening heaven.

—RABINDRANATH TAGORE

Trees! I come to you! To save myself
From the roar of the marketplace.
How my heart breathes out
Through your flights upward!

—MARINA TSVETAYEVA

☾ understanding

Sit down before fact as a little child, be prepared to give up every preconceived notion, follow humbly wherever and to whatever abyss nature leads, or you shall learn nothing.

—THOMAS H. HUXLEY

The whole visible world is only an imperceptible atom in the ample bosom of nature. No idea approaches it.

—BLAISE PASCAL

Nature is always hinting at us. It hints over and over again. And suddenly we take the hint.

—ROBERT FROST

A bird does not sing because it has an answer—it sings because it has a song.

— CHINESE PROVERB

Our knowledge is a receding mirage in an expanding desert of ignorance.

— WILL DURANT

In my twenties I regarded the universe as an open book full of mathematical formulae. And now I regard it as an invisible piece of writing in which we can now and then decipher a letter or a word and then it's gone again.

— ARTHUR KOESTLER

I'm astounded by people who want to "know" the universe when it's hard enough to find your way around Chinatown.

— WOODY ALLEN

The only solid piece of scientific truth about which I feel totally confident is that we are profoundly ignorant about nature. . . . It is this sudden confrontation with the depth and scope of ignorance that represents the most significant contribution of twentieth-century science to the human intellect.

—LEWIS THOMAS

❰ universe

The universe begins to look more like a great thought than like a great machine.

—SIR JAMES JEANS

I do not value any view of the universe into which man and the institutions of man enter very largely and absorb much of the attention. Man is but the place where I stand, and the prospect hence is infinite.

—HENRY DAVID THOREAU

Overhead the sanctities of the stars shine forevermore . . . pouring satire on the pompous business of the day which they close, and making the generations of men show slight and evanescent.

—RALPH WALDO EMERSON

They cannot scare me with their empty spaces
Between stars—on stars where no human
  race is.
I have it in me so much nearer home
To scare myself with my own desert places.

—ROBERT FROST

[The universe:] The most exquisite
masterpiece ever composed by nobody.

—G. K. CHESTERTON

  (attributed)

If we could count the stars, we should
not weep before them.

—GEORGE SANTAYANA

☾ warnings

Woe unto them that join house to house, that lay field to field; till there be no place, that they may be placed alone in the midst of the earth!

—BIBLE, *ISAIAH* 5:8

The ground is holy ... Keep it, guard it, care for it, for it keeps men, guards men, cares for men. Destroy it and man is destroyed.

—ALAN PATON

We are cutting out our kidneys to enlarge our stomachs.

—ERIC FREYFOGLE

(on the destruction of wetlands)

Man can achieve some form of tolerance to environmental pollution, excessive environmental stimuli, crowded and competitive social contacts, the estrangement of life from the natural biological cycles, and other consequences of life in the urban and technological world. . . . But in many cases, it is achieved through organic and mental processes which may result in the chronic and degenerative disorders that so commonly spoil adult life and old age, even in the most prosperous countries.

— RENÉ DUBOS

Social systems which have not been in harmony with the natural system, which have demanded more of it than it could deliver without undue stress, or that have taken from it more than they returned, have not, historically, survived for any great length of time.

— PAUL GRUCHOW

Today every inhabitant of this planet must contemplate the day when this planet may no longer be habitable. Every man, woman and child lives under a nuclear sword of Damocles, hanging by the slenderest of threads, capable of being cut at any moment by accident or miscalculation or madness.

—JOHN F. KENNEDY

We, the generation that faces the next century, can add the . . . solemn injunction "If we don't do the impossible, we shall be faced with the unthinkable."

—PETRA KELLY

Once, perhaps, the God-intoxicated few could abscond to the wild frontiers, the forests, the desert places to keep alive the perennial wisdom that they harbored. But no longer. They must now become a political force or their tradition perishes. Soon enough, there will be no solitude left for the saints to roam but its air will shudder with the noise of great engines that drowns out all prayers.

—THEODORE ROSZAK

Your salvation is in your own hands . . . Nature is indifferent to the survival of the human species, including Americans. She does not weep over those who fall by the way.

—ADLAI E. STEVENSON

Pity the meek for they shall inherit the earth.

—DON MARQUIS

We have been massively intervening in the environment without being aware of many of the harmful consequences of our acts. . . . Like the sorcerer's apprentice, we are acting upon dangerously incomplete knowledge. We are, in effect, conducting a huge experiment on *ourselves.*

— BARRY COMMONER

Without a global revolution in the sphere of human consciousness, nothing will change for the better in the sphere of our being as humans, and the catastrophe toward which this world is headed—be it ecological, social, demographic or a general breakdown of civilization—will be unavoidable.

— VACLAV HAVEL

Unless we change direction, we are likely to end up where we are headed.

— CHINESE PROVERB

☾ weather

A change in the weather is sufficient to recreate the world and ourselves.

—MARCEL PROUST

Sunshine is delicious, rain is refreshing, wind braces us up, snow is exhilarating; there's really no such thing as bad weather, only different kinds of good weather.

—JOHN RUSKIN

Nothing is so beautiful as spring—
When weeds, in wheels, shoot long and
    lovely and lush;
Thrush's eggs look little low heavens,
    and thrush
Through the echoing timber does so rinse
    and wring
The ear, it strikes like lightning to hear
    him sing.

— GERARD MANLEY HOPKINS

Under my tree-roof
Slanting lines of April rain
Separate to drops.

— BASHŌ

Rain! whose soft architectural hands
have power to cut stones, and chisel to shapes of
grandeur the very mountains.

— HENRY WARD BEECHER

*I am the Poem of the Earth, said the voice of
   the rain,
Eternal I rise impalpable out of the land and
   the bottomless sea.*

—WALT WHITMAN

What a thing it is to sit absolutely
alone, in the forest at night, cherished by this
wonderful, unintelligible, perfectly innocent
speech, the most comforting speech in the
world, the talk that rain makes by itself all over
the ridges, and the talk of the watercourses
everywhere in the hollows!

Nobody started it, nobody is going to
stop it. It will talk as long as it wants, this rain.
As long as it talks I am going to listen.

—THOMAS MERTON

Thank heaven, the sun has gone in, and I don't have to go out and enjoy it.

—LOGAN PEARSALL SMITH

The day of the sun is like the day of a king. It is a promenade in the morning, a sitting on the throne at noon, a pageant in the evening.

—WALLACE STEVENS

The sun was like a great visiting presence that stimulated and took its due from all animal energy. When it flung down its cloak and stepped down over the edge of the fields at evening, it left behind it a spent and exhausted world.

—WILLA CATHER

The Sun, the hearth of affection and
life, pours burning love on the delighted earth.

—ARTHUR RIMBAUD

Praise be to Thee, my Lord, for Brother
    Wind,
And for the air and the cloud of fair and all
    weather
Through which Thou givest sustenance to
    Thy creatures.

—FRANCIS OF ASSISI

There's a certain slant of light,
On winter afternoons,
That oppresses, like the weight
Of cathedral tunes.

—EMILY DICKINSON

In the bleak mid-winter
Frosty wind made moan,
Earth stood hard as iron,
Water like a stone;
Snow had fallen, snow on snow,
Snow on snow,
In the bleak mid-winter,
Long ago.

—CHRISTINA ROSSETTI

☾ wilderness

It is a joy to contemplate Cytorus asurge
with box-trees and the firwoods of Narycus, a
joy also to see fields indebted to no drag-hoes or
human care.

—VIRGIL

Besides, what could they see but a
hideous and desolate wilderness, full of wild
beasts and wild men? And what multitudes there
might be of them they knew not.

—WILLIAM BRADFORD

*(the Pilgrim leader's view of the New England
"wilderness" in 1622)*

We did not think of the great open plains, the beautiful rolling hills, and winding streams with tangled growth as "wild." Only to the white man was nature a "wilderness" and only to him was the land "infested" with "wild" animals and "savage" people. To us it was tame. Earth was plentiful and we were surrounded with the blessings of the Great Mystery.

—CHIEF LUTHER STANDING BEAR

What would the world be once bereft
Of wet and wildness? Let them be left,
O let them be left, wildness and wet;
Long live the weeds and the wilderness yet.

—GERARD MANLEY HOPKINS

The clearest way into the universe is through a forest wilderness.

—JOHN MUIR

I love all waste
And solitary places; where we taste the
   pleasure of believing what we see
Is boundless, as we wish our souls to be.

—PERCY BYSSHE SHELLEY

Hope and the future for me are
not in lawns and cultivated fields, not in
towns and cities, but in the impervious and
quaking swamps.

—HENRY DAVID THOREAU

In wildness is the preservation of
the world.

—HENRY DAVID THOREAU

We need the tonic of wildness—to wade sometimes in marshes where the bittern and the meadow-hen lurk, and hear the booming of the snipe; to smell the whispering sedge where only some wilder and more solitary fowl builds her nest, and the mink crawls with its belly close to the ground.

— HENRY DAVID THOREAU

Sweet is the swamp with its secrets,
Until we meet a snake;
'Tis then we sigh for houses,
And our departure take.

— EMILY DICKINSON

Leave it as it is. The ages have been at work on it and man can only mar it.

— THEODORE ROOSEVELT

(speaking about the Grand Canyon, 1903)

Man always kills the things he loves, and so we the pioneers have killed our wilderness. Some say we had to. Be that as it may, I am glad I shall never be young without wild country to be young in. Of what avail are forty freedoms without a blank spot on the map?

—ALDO LEOPOLD

There is clearly not enough wilderness left for the rising number of people who say they desire it. It's not wilderness anyway if it only exists by our permission and stewardship. The famous Thoreau quote said "wildness" not wilderness. We have become Europe and each, with a sense of privacy and tact, must secure our own wildness.

—JIM HARRISON

To me, a wilderness is where the flow of wildness is essentially uninterrupted by technology; without wilderness, the world's a cage.

—DAVID BOWER

Without any remaining wilderness we are committed wholly, without chance for even momentary reflection and rest, to a headlong drive into our technological termite-life, the Brave New World of completely man-controlled environment. We need wilderness preserved—as much of it as is still left, and as many kinds—because it was the challenge against which our character as a people was formed. The reminder and the reassurance that it is still there is good for our spiritual health even if we never once in ten years set foot in it. It is good for us when we are young, because of the incomparable sanity it can bring briefly, as vacation and rest, into our insane lives. It is important to us when we are old simply because it is there—important, that is, simply as idea.

—WALLACE STEGNER

☾ wonder

The first act of awe when man was struck with the beauty or wonder of nature was the first spiritual experience.

—HENRYK SKOLIMOWSKI

To become human, one must make room in oneself for the wonders of the universe.

—SOUTH AMERICAN INDIAN SAYING

I do not wonder at a snowflake, a shell, a summer landscape, or the glory of the stars; but at the necessity of beauty under which the universe lies.

—RALPH WALDO EMERSON

The cow crunching with depressed head
surpasses any statue,
And a mouse is miracle enough to stagger
sextillions of infidels.

—WALT WHITMAN

O amazement of things—even the least
particle!

—WALT WHITMAN

If I had influence with the good fairy who is supposed to preside over the christening of all children I should ask that her gift to each child in the world be a sense of wonder so indestructible that it would last throughout life, as an unfailing antidote against the boredom and disenchantments of later years, the sterile preoccupation with things that are artificial, the alienation from the sources of our strength.

—RACHEL CARSON

Soon the child's clear eye is clouded over by ideas and opinions, preconceptions and abstractions. Simple free being becomes encrusted with the burdensome armor of the ego. Not until years later does an instinct come that a vital sense of mystery has been withdrawn. The sun glints through the pines, and the heart is pierced in a moment of beauty and strange pain, like a memory of paradise. After that day . . . we become seekers.

— PETER MATTHIESSEN

There is not a sprig of grass that shoots uninteresting to me, nor any thing that moves.

— THOMAS JEFFERSON

We see as fine risings of the sun as ever Adam saw; and its risings are as much a miracle now as they were in his day . . .

—DANIEL WEBSTER

One thing I'd like to know most of all: when those ants have made the Hill, and are all there, touching and exchanging, and the whole mass begins to behave like a single huge creature, and *thinks*, what on earth is that thought? And while you're at it, I'd like to know a second thing: when it happens, does any single ant know about it? Does his hair stand on end?

—LEWIS THOMAS

The grand show is eternal. It is always sunrise somewhere; the dew is never all dried at once; a shower is forever falling; vapor is ever rising. Eternal sunrise, eternal sunset, eternal dawn and gloaming, on sea and continents and islands, each in its turn, as the round earth rolls.

—JOHN MUIR

❨ editor's note

As extensive as this collection is, some readers will notice the absence of a favorite quotation. If you have one you'd like to see included in a future edition, please send it (with the source, so it can be verified) to Birch Tree Publishing, 100 Russian Village Rd., Southbury, CT 06488.

thomas willoughby nason

Thomas Willoughby Nason, the man who made the superb engravings printed in this book, was born in Dracut, Massachusetts in 1889. During his career he won more than fifty awards in exhibitions around the world. He was commissioned to illustrate fine editions of Thoreau's *Walden* and the poems of his friend Robert Frost. Samuel Palmer, a fellow artist, said of Nason: "His execution is of that highest order which has no independent essence, but lingers and hesitates with the thought, and is lost and found in a bewilderment of intricate beauty." Nason concentrated on making wood and copper engravings until, in his seventies, his eyes became too weak to produce the finely detailed work for which he was known. He died in 1971 at the age of 82.

❛ index

(Including suggestions for further reading)